WHAT A WORLD 3

SECOND EDITION

READING

Amazing Stories
from Around the Globe

Milada Broukal

PEARSON
Longman

D0083996

What a World Reading 3: Amazing Stories from Around the Globe

Copyright © 2011 by Pearson Education, Inc.
All rights reserved. No part of this publication may be reproduced, stored in a retrieval system, or transmitted in any form or by any means, electronic, mechanical, photocopying, recording, or otherwise, without the prior permission of the publisher.

Pearson Education, 10 Bank Street, White Plains, NY 10606

Staff credits: The people who made up the *What a World Reading 3* team, representing editorial, production, design, and manufacturing, are Pietro Alongi, Rhea Banker, John Barnes, John Brezinsky, Aerin Csigay, Mindy DePalma, Nancy Flaggman, Amy McCormick, Linda Moser, Jennifer Stem, and Patricia Wosczyk.
Cover and text design: Patricia Wosczyk
Text composition: ElectraGraphics, Inc.
Text font: Minion
Photo Credits: Page 1 iStockphoto.com; p. 11 Shutterstock.com; p. 21 Photos India/Photolibrary.com; p. 30 The Art Archive/Alamy; p. 39 Shutterstock.com; p. 50 Rene Wouters/Alamy; p. 59 Shutterstock.com; p. 69 Shutterstock.com; p. 82 Jacques Alexandre/age fotostock; p. 92 National Geographic/Getty Images; p. 103 Shutterstock.com; p. 113 Shutterstock.com; p. 123 Shutterstock.com; p. 133 Photolibrary.com; p. 142 Hulton-Deutsch Collection/Corbis; p. 152 Andrew Brusso/Corbis.

Library of Congress Cataloging-in-Publication Data
Library of Congress Cataloging-in-Publication Data

Broukal, Milada.
   What a world reading: amazing stories from around the globe / Milada Broukal.—2nd ed.
      p. cm —(What a world reading : amazing stories from around the globe series)
   Includes index.
   Previous ed.: 2004.
   ISBN 0-13-247267-8 (u.1)—ISBN 0-13-247796-3 (u.2)—ISBN 0-13-138201-2 (u.3) 1. English language—Textbooks for foreign speakers. 2. Readers—Manners and customs.
   PE1128.B7165 2010
   428.6'4—dc22

2010020089

ISBN-13: 978-0-13-1382015
ISBN-10: 0-13-138201-2

PEARSON LONGMAN ON THE WEB

Pearsonlongman.com offers online resources for teachers and students. Access our Companion Websites, our online catalog, and our local offices around the world.

Visit us at **www.pearsonlongman.com**.

Printed in the United States of America
1 2 3 4 5 6 7 8 9 10–V011–19 18 17 16 15 14 13 12 11 10

CONTENTS

INTRODUCTION

The *What a World: Amazing Stories from Around the Globe* series

This series now has two strands: a reading strand and a listening strand. Both strands explore linked topics from around the world and across history. They can be used separately or together for maximum exploration of content and development of essential reading and listening skills.

	Reading Strand	**Listening Strand**
Level 1 (Beginning)	*What a World Reading 1, 2e*	*What a World Listening 1*
Level 2 (High-Beginning)	*What a World Reading 2, 2e*	*What a World Listening 2*
Level 3 (Intermediate)	*What a World Reading 3, 2e*	*What a World Listening 3*

What a World Reading 3, 2e is an intermediate reader.

It is the third in a three-book series of readings for English language learners. The sixteen units in this book correspond thematically with the units in *What a World Listening 3*. Each topic is about a different person, people, place, custom, or organization. The topics span history and the globe, from life in a medieval castle, to Angkor Wat, to the story of tea.

What is special about the Second Edition of *What a World Reading 3?*

- New and updated readings: there are five new readings
- Critical thinking questions have been added in every unit to develop students' thinking skills
- Internet Activities have been added for every unit to build students' Internet research skills; these activities are in the Appendices at the back of the book.

What is in a Unit and how does it work?

Every unit begins with a question and answers that question. Each unit contains:

- A prereading activity
- A reading passage (900–1200 words)
- Topic-related vocabulary work
- Comprehension exercises, including pair work
- Discussion questions
- Critical thinking questions
- A writing activity
- Grammar and punctuation activities

Unit Structure and Approach

BEFORE YOU READ opens with a picture of the person, people, place, custom, or organization featured in the unit. Prereading questions follow. Their purpose is to motivate students to read, encourage predictions about the content of the reading, and involve the students' own experiences when possible. Vocabulary can be presented as the need arises.

READING passages should first be done individually by skimming for the general content. The teacher may wish to explain the bolded vocabulary words at this point. The students should then do a second, closer reading. Further reading(s) can be done aloud.

VOCABULARY exercises focus on the boldfaced words in the reading. There are three types of vocabulary exercises. Both *Meaning* and *Words That Go Together* are definition exercises that encourage students to work out the meanings of words from the context. *Meaning* focuses on single words, *Words That Go Together* focuses on collocations or groups of words which are easier to learn together the way they are used in the language. The third exercise, *Use*, reinforces the vocabulary further by making students use the words or collocations in a meaningful, yet possibly different, context. This section can be done during or after the reading phase, or both.

COMPREHENSION exercises appear in each unit and consist of *Understanding Main Ideas*, *Remembering Details*, and *Making Inferences*. All confirm the content of the text either in general or in detail. These exercises for developing reading skills can be done individually, in pairs, in small groups, or as a class. It is preferable to do these exercises in conjunction with the text, since they are not meant to test memory.

DISCUSSION questions encourage students to bring their own ideas and imagination to the related topics in each reading. They can also provide insights into cultural similarities and differences.

CRITICAL THINKING questions give students the opportunity to develop thinking skills (comparing and contrasting cultural customs, recognizing personal attitudes and values, etc.)

WRITING provides the stimulus for students to write paragraphs or essays about the reading. Teachers should use their own discretion when deciding whether or not to correct the writing exercises.

GRAMMAR AND PUNCTUATION exercises provide basic rules and accompanying activities for grammar or punctuation, using examples from the readings.

Additional Activities

INTERNET ACTIVITIES (in the Appendices) give students the opportunity to develop their Internet research skills. Each activity can be done in a classroom setting or if the students have Internet Access, as homework leading to a presentation or discussion in class. There is an Internet activity for each unit and it is always related to the theme of the unit. It helps students evaluate websites for their reliability and gets them to process and put together the information in an organized way.

SELF-TESTS after Unit 8 and Unit 16 review comprenhension, vocabulary, and grammar and punctuation in a multiple-choice format.

＊＊＊＊＊

If you would like the **Answer Key** for *What a World Reading 3, 2e*, please go to the following website: http://www.pearsonlongman.com/whataworld.

WHAT WAS LIFE LIKE IN A MEDIEVAL CASTLE?

you read

Answer these questions.

before

1. Why did people build castles in the old days?
2. What did castles look like inside and out?
3. What do you think life was like inside a castle 700 years ago?

WHAT WAS LIFE LIKE IN A MEDIEVAL CASTLE?

1   Many of us dream about living in a castle, mainly because movies have made them glamorous. In reality, life was not easy or comfortable in a castle, especially in medieval times. *Medieval* comes from Latin and means "middle age." The period between 500 and 1500 is sometimes referred to as the Middle Ages because it came between the Roman world and modern times. During this period, castles were cold, damp places with **draughts** because the windows had no glass. Castles had no central heating; there was only a big fire in the hall and one in the kitchen. There was no running water or toilets, either. A castle, however, did have something that people needed most—protection!

2   In the beginning, castles were made of wood and were usually located on a hill. They often had a deep, wide hole, or moat, around them, filled with water for protection against enemies. Wooden castles were not very strong and **caught fire** easily and were soon **replaced by** stone buildings. Later on, stone castles needed more protection, so outer walls with a special gate and towers were built. Inside the castle walls, there were various buildings. There was a chapel for prayer, stables for the horses, workshops for craftsmen, a mill for making flour, an armory to keep weapons, dungeons to keep prisoners, and a guard room for soldiers. There were also gardens for growing fruits and vegetables and a well to provide fresh water. Finally, the largest building standing in the middle of the castle was the "keep." It was here that one found the great hall and the lord's private rooms. With the outer walls, towers, and soldiers protecting them, people within the castle felt safe against enemy attack.

3   The great hall was the center of castle life. The lord **carried out** his daily business and met with people there. It even became a courtroom to punish people who **broke the law**. The walls had tapestries on them to keep out the cold. At mealtimes, long tables were put in the great hall. Breakfast was at sunrise and consisted of bread and wine or ale, and the main meal of the day was served between 10 A.M. and noon. The lord and his family were seated at a "high table" on a **raised** platform. From here he could look down on the lower members of his **household** sitting at the "low" tables. Guests were seated in order of importance, starting with church members, noblemen, and then the lord's family. If they had important guests, there might be minstrels, who sang songs, jugglers, or even acrobats, for entertainment between **courses**. The lord was served first, after a servant sampled his food to make sure it was not poisoned. After this, family members and guests were served. Food was carried from the kitchen to the table so it was served very hot. There were no forks at the time, so people ate with their fingers. Important men carried their own knives with them. A very important

guest would have his own glass for wine placed on the table for him, but other guests shared their cups of wine with the person sitting next to them. They also shared their plates of food. Those who did not share plates ate on a *trencher*, which was a slice of **stale** bread. This **soaked up** the juice and fat of the food. When they finished eating, they gave the trenchers to the poor, who were waiting outside the castle gates. Table etiquette was strict since people ate with their fingers. One writer's advice was, "If it happens that you cannot help scratching, then courteously take a portion of your dress, and scratch with that."

4   Early medieval castles usually had only one bedroom. This private room was for the lord and his family, usually next to the great hall. They were the only people who had beds to sleep on because a bed was an expensive item. The rest of the household slept in the hall, which was the warmest place, especially if there was a fire burning there during the day. Tables would be put away against the walls, and **mattresses** filled with **straw** would be put down on the floor. Many people would sleep on the same mattress. People who worked in certain parts of the castle would sleep where they worked; for example, cooks slept in the kitchen.

5   The kitchen was usually in a separate part of the castle in case it caught fire. Many people worked in the kitchen. Young boys had the job of fetching water from the well and cleaning the cauldron, or big pot, that hung from a hook over an open fire. People in the castle ate whatever the farmers brought them, as well as what they could hunt. When food was plentiful, they had pork, mutton, poultry, and fish. From the forest, they brought in venison, wild pig, and wild birds. Meat often went bad quickly because there was no refrigeration, so they salted it. To **disguise** the taste of **rotten** meat, cooks used a lot of spices from the East, which poorer people could not afford. People ate a lot of bread and some vegetables such as beans, peas, and turnips. Potatoes had not come to Europe at that time. Honey was used to sweeten food and drink, and some castles even kept honey bees.

6   As can be seen, castle life in medieval times was not comfortable and certainly wasn't clean, since clean water was not **readily available**. Not much importance was given to cleanliness and **privacy**. Straw was put on the floors, which were made of earth or stone, and rarely **swept out**. Since dogs and cats lived among the people in the castle, and everyone slept, ate, and lived on the straw, one can only imagine what was in it. As for privacy, only the lord and his family had a private space. The rest of the household lived in open areas. The servants had a hard life since everything was made and done by hand. So the next time you dream of living in a castle, think twice. It's one dream you might not want to come true.

VOCABULARY

MEANING

Circle the letter of the answer that is closest in meaning to the underlined word.

1. Castles were cold, damp places with <u>draughts</u>.
   a. air flowing through a room
   b. water coming in from outside
   c. smoke coming into a room
   d. sun heating up a room

2. The lord and his family sat at a "high table" on a <u>raised</u> platform.
   a. made lower
   b. made even with
   c. made higher
   d. made larger

3. He could look down on the lower members of his <u>household</u>.
   a. people living together in a house
   b. anyone working in a house
   c. the older members of a family
   d. the owners of a house

4. They had acrobats for entertainment between <u>courses</u>.
   a. conversations
   b. forms of entertainment
   c. subjects of study
   d. parts of a meal

5. A *trencher* was a slice of <u>stale</u> bread.
   a. just baked
   b. no longer fresh
   c. white and thin
   d. dark and thick

6. <u>Mattresses</u> filled with straw would be put down on the floor.
   a. large wooden boxes for sleeping on
   b. large bags of material for sleeping on
   c. raised platforms for sleeping on
   d. large sacks of cloth for sleeping inside of

7. Mattresses filled with <u>straw</u> would be put down on the floor.
   a. cut up pieces of rough cloth
   b. sand taken from the banks of a river
   c. dried stems of grain plants
   d. leaves and grass mixed together

8. To <u>disguise</u> the taste of rotten meat, cooks used a lot of spices.
   a. increase
   b. hide
   c. improve
   d. keep

9. To disguise the taste of <u>rotten</u> meat, cooks used a lot of spices.
   a. very fresh
   b. salty
   c. no longer good
   d. overcooked

10. Not much importance was given to cleanliness and <u>privacy</u>.
    a. being with other people
    b. sharing things with other people
    c. having more rights than other people
    d. being separated from other people

WORDS THAT GO TOGETHER

A. *Find words in the reading that go together with the words below to make phrases.*

1. carried _____

2. _____ available

(continued)

3. soaked _____

4. _____ fire

5. _____ the law

6. swept _____

7. replaced _____

B. *Complete the sentences with the phrases from Part A.*

1. If something _____ a liquid, it drew the liquid into itself.

2. When actions or duties are _____, they are performed or accomplished.

3. If you changed one thing for another, the first thing was _____ the second.

4. When something began to burn, it _____.

5. If something is _____, it is close by for someone to use or have.

6. If you _____ an area, you removed dirt or other things with a broom or brush.

7. If a person went against the rules set by a governing body, he or she _____.

C. *Now use the phrases in your own sentences.*

EXAMPLE: *After lightning struck a tree, the forest* caught fire.

USE

Work with a partner to answer the questions. Use complete sentences.

1. Where can you see a *raised* stage?
2. Of all the dinner *courses*, which do you like best?
3. What is something you do to have *privacy*?
4. Do you like to sleep on a hard or soft *mattress*?
5. How do we know when bread is *stale*?
6. Who are the members of your *household*?
7. What is a food that goes *rotten* quickly?
8. What is one use for *straw*?

COMPREHENSION

UNDERSTANDING MAIN IDEAS

Some of the following statements are main ideas and some are supporting statements. Some of them are stated directly in the reading. Find the statements. Write M for each main idea. Write S for each supporting statement.

1. _____ Life in a castle was not easy or comfortable..

2. _____ Castles had many buildings for various uses inside the castle walls.

3. _____ At the main meal, the household was seated, served, entertained, and ate according to custom.

4. _____ Medieval castles usually had only one bedroom.

5. _____ The household ate various farmed foods, fish, and meat from the forest prepared by the kitchen servants.

REMEMBERING DETAILS

Reread the passage and answer the questions. Write complete sentences.

1. Where does the word *medieval* come from?

   _____

2. What was the "keep" of the castle?

   _____

3. Why did a servant sample the lord's food?

   _____

4. What did household members do with trenchers after they had finished eating?

   _____

5. Why were the lord and his family the only people who had beds?

   _____

6. Why was the kitchen built in a separate area of the castle?

   _____

7. What did the household eat when food was plentiful on the farms?

   _____

8. What was honey used for?

   _____

MAKING INFERENCES

The answers to these questions can be inferred, or guessed, from the reading. Circle the letter of the best answer.

1. It can be inferred from the reading that people in medieval times _____.
   a. lived comfortable and peaceful lives
   b. lived in a dangerous time
   c. had the protection of strong laws by an organized government
   d. were quite healthy and strong

2. The reading implies that in the castle _____.
   a. there were all the things necessary for a comfortable life
   b. everyone lived their lives in the same level of comfort
   c. people generally lived healthy and carefree lives
   d. items of comfort and even necessity were very few

3. From the reading, it can be concluded that the lord of the castle _____.
   a. provided for the basic needs of his household
   b. caused great suffering to the members of his household
   c. could not protect all the members of his household
   d. considered himself equal to all the members of his household

4. The reading implies that _____.
   a. everyone inside and outside the castle had plenty of food
   b. people in the household often didn't have enough food
   c. the quantity of the food didn't necessarily match the quality
   d. people at that time didn't know how to cook food very well

DISCUSSION

Discuss the answers to these questions with your classmates.

1. What were the advantages and disadvantages of living in a castle?
2. Not all the lords of castles were alike. What do you think a good lord was like? What do you think a bad lord was like? What kind of lord (or mistress) would you have been? What would you have done for the people of your household?
3. What are the differences between castles today and castles in medieval times? Would you like to live in a castle? Why or why not?

4. A servant tasted the lord's food to make sure it wasn't poisoned. Who might want to poison a lord and why? What do you think of the practice of having a servant taste the food? What does it tell us about the attitude toward servants in those days?

CRITICAL THINKING

Work with a partner. Ask each other the following questions. Discuss your answers.

1. In medieval times, there was a servant class and an upper class. What problems arise in a society in which there are only "haves" and "have-nots"? What are some examples from history? Why does having a large middle class ensure stability in society? What are some countries today that have a society of "haves" and "have-nots"? What are some countries that have a large middle class?

2. What do people need protection from today? What measures do we take to protect ourselves in our homes and personal lives?

WRITING

On a separate piece of paper, write a paragraph or an essay about one of the following topics.

1. Write about a perfect place to live.
2. Write about two or three things you protect yourself against. Give reasons.
3. What are the advantages and/or disadvantages of having security cameras on streets for our protection?

GRAMMAR AND PUNCTUATION

SUBJECT–VERB AGREEMENT

1. A singular subject takes a singular verb, and a plural subject takes a plural verb.
   The great hall was the center of castle life.
   In the beginning, castles were made of wood.
   Two subjects joined by and take a plural verb.
   The lord and his family were seated at a "high table."

2. Words between the subject and the verb do not change subject–verb agreement.
   The castle of the lord of the manor and his family was the most important building in the village. (The subject is "the castle," not "the lord of the manor and his family.")

(continued)

> Phrases such as *together with*, *as well as*, and *accompanied by* do not change the subject–verb agreement.
> ***The castle**, as well as all its buildings, **is protected** by soldiers.*
>
> 3. When a sentence starts with *there*, the verb must agree with the subject that follows.
> *There **was a** big **fire** in the hall.*
> *There **were** no **forks** at the time.*

Underline the correct form of the verb in parentheses.

1. The lord and his family (was / were) the only ones who had a private room.

2. The stone castle with its towers (was / were) located on top of the hill.

3. The moat, as well as the towers, (was / were) important for the protection of the building.

4. In the middle of the castle, there (was / were) a "keep."

5. There (were / was) other buildings in the castle, too.

6. The medieval castle, with all its romance, (was / were) not a comfortable place to live.

7. There (is / are) many medieval castles still standing today.

8. The medieval castle (has / have) been glamorized in movies.

9. The Queen of England, accompanied by her staff, still (live / lives) in Windsor castle for certain months of the year.

10. The combination of history and romance (make / makes) a castle attractive to tourists today.

🖱 *Go to page 167 for the Internet Activity.*

Go to page 167 for the Internet Activity.

| DID YOU KNOW? | • Almost all castles had a well within their walls. Having water was important if the enemy surrounded the castle.
• When enemies attacked, soldiers poured hot water onto the heads of the enemy through holes in the castle walls.
• Castles had a mill for making flour.
• Round towers were stronger than square towers because they did not have weak corners. Not all towers were round, but they became more and more popular. |

WHY DID THE INCA EMPIRE DISAPPEAR?

before

you read

Answer these questions.

1. Who were the earliest people to settle in your country? What do you know about them?
2. How long ago do you think the Incas lived?
3. In what part of the world do you think the Incas lived?

WHY DID THE INCA EMPIRE DISAPPEAR?

1   The land of the Incas included what is now Bolivia, Peru, Ecuador, and part of Argentina and Chile. In the center of the Inca Empire was its capital, Cuzco, the "Sacred City of the Sun." From every part of the empire, grain, gold and silver, cloth, and food poured into the capital.

2   The Incas began as a small tribe living in the Peruvian Andes in the 1100s. In the 1300s, their strong leader, Mayta Qapaq, began to conquer neighboring lands. By the 1400s, the Incas' huge empire became the largest empire known in the Americas. Although there were only 40,000 Incas, they ruled a population of about 12 million, which included 100 different peoples. The Incas were clever governors and did not always force their own ideas on other groups. The people they conquered had to accept the Inca gods, but they were **allowed** to worship in their own way and keep their own customs.

3   Each new ruler of the empire was called the Sapa Inca, and each Sapa Inca **claimed** to be the child of the sun and was treated as a god. When a Sapa Inca died, his body was kept and taken care of by the people, and he continued to "live" in his palace. The dead Inca sat on a golden stool, and a woman watched him day and night, whisking the flies away from his face. The dead rulers were served food each day, and **on special occasions** they were carried out of their palaces to feast together. Each new ruler had to build a new palace. By 1500, Cuzco was full of palaces of dead Incas.

4   Each Sapa Inca had a queen, or Coya. She was almost always the ruler's own sister. Like him, she was thought to be a child of the sun. The Sapa Inca married his sister to make sure their children only had the pure blood of the sun. One of their sons would be the next Sapa Inca. However, each Sapa Inca had many unofficial wives and dozens of children who would become the Inca nobility.

5   The Incas ruled over one of the best organized empires in history. They controlled the lives of everyone through a system of officials. This system was like a triangle or pyramid. At the bottom were millions of ordinary farmers. Above the farmers were officials and higher officials, and above these officials were the four governors of the quarters of the empire. At the very top of the pyramid was the Sapa Inca.

6   Ordinary people had to spend part of each year working for the state—mining, building roads, or **serving in the army**. They could not leave their villages without official permission. They had no choice but to work on the land and send one-third of their produce to the government storehouses. The empire had huge storehouses where food was kept. The Incas made sure no one **starved**. In return, everyone was expected to work.

7   Even marriage of the ordinary people was controlled. Although nobles often had several wives, an ordinary man could only have one. The state controlled whom and when each ordinary person could marry. Each year, the local chiefs assembled all the **eligible** young men over twenty-four and women over eighteen. They were grouped into two lines and then paired together. For the first year of marriage, the couple did not have to pay taxes on either goods or labor. However, they would have to work hard for the rest of their lives. When they were elderly and became too **frail** or sick to take care of themselves, they received free food and clothes from the state storehouse, and their family groups would care for them.

8   The Incas had no horses or wheels to help them with transportation, but they had a **sophisticated** road system. Their network of roads ran the length of the empire, from today's Peru to Chile. One road, called the Royal Road, was 3,250 miles (5,200 km) long. It was built through the Andes Mountains. Even today, with modern tools, it would be difficult to build that road. The Incas also made extraordinary suspension bridges of ropes; these hung 300 feet (91 meters) above deep rivers. Since most people were not allowed to travel, the roads were used by soldiers and *chasquis*, who were government messengers. They were highly trained runners who were stationed **at intervals** of about 2 miles (3.2 km) along the roads and carried messages to and from Cuzco. Relay teams could run up to 200 miles (322 km) a day and bring fish from the sea to the capital in two days. But the main reason for the roads was for the soldiers who kept the empire **under control**.

9   Although they had no system of writing, the Incas sent messages in *quipus*, which were colored strings with **knots** in them. The color of the string represented what was being counted. For example, a yellow string **stood for** gold and a red string for soldiers. The knots stood for numbers.

10   The Incas were expert builders, although they only had basic tools. Instead of building walls with cement, they used stones that fit together perfectly. Many of the Inca walls remain in place to this day. In 1950, two-thirds of Cuzco was destroyed in an earthquake, but none of the old walls **collapsed**. Today the well-preserved town of Machu Picchu shows the remarkable skills of the Inca builders. This town, which was **abandoned** by the Incas for unknown reasons, was only discovered in 1911.

11   The Inca Empire fell very quickly after the death of their great ruler Huayna Capac in 1525. Two of his sons, Atahualpa and Huascar, quarreled over who should be the next Sapa Inca. They fought against each other in a war, and finally, in 1532, Atahualpa won. During the war, news came that strange people had arrived on the coast. These visitors, the Spaniards, were dressed in metal suits, rode unknown animals (horses), and had hair growing down their chins. After his victory, Atahualpa wanted to see these strange people and invited them to visit him. There were only 180 Spaniards, so Atahualpa was not afraid. However, the Spaniards attacked the Inca army with guns and fired their cannons. They took Atahualpa prisoner and promised

(continued)

to give him his freedom **in exchange for** a room full of gold and two rooms full of silver. The Incas gave the Spaniards the gold and silver. However, the Spaniards didn't free Atahualpa; they killed him instead. With no leader, the Inca soldiers were weak, and the Spaniards soon defeated them. The Spaniards gave the Incas orders, and the Incas obeyed them because they were used to obeying all their lives. The Spaniards were only interested in the Inca gold and silver, so they made the people work in the mines and **neglect** the farming. Many Incas died from overwork and hunger. The great Inca Empire was soon destroyed.

12   Though the Inca civilization disappeared, traces of its culture and people survive. As a matter of fact, today, the Incas' descendants form the **majority of** the population in the Andes of Ecuador and Bolivia.

VOCABULARY

MEANING

Circle the letter of the answer that is closest in meaning to the underlined word.

1. The Incas had a <u>sophisticated</u> road system.
   a. not well developed
   b. plain and simple
   c. advanced and complicated
   d. roughly put together

2. Each Sapa Inca <u>claimed</u> to be a child of the sun.
   a. stated as a fact
   b. showed to be untrue
   c. questioned the truth of
   d. demanded to know

3. They were <u>allowed</u> to worship in their own way.
   a. forced
   b. forbidden
   c. told how
   d. given permission

4. They made the people work in the mines and <u>neglect</u> the farming.
   a. not take care of
   b. take care of
   c. do more of
   d. watch over

5. Machu Picchu was <u>abandoned</u> by the Incas.
   a. torn down
   b. left empty or alone
   c. made more beautiful
   d. built up

6. The Incas made sure that no one underlined{starved}.
   a. had food
   c. was forced to buy food
   b. went without food
   d. stored food

7. When they became too _frail_ or sick to take care of themselves, they received free food and clothes.
   a. completely unhappy
   c. poor and hungry
   b. lonely and afraid
   d. thin and weak

8. None of the old Inca walls underlined{collapsed}.
   a. had large cracks
   c. were damaged
   b. fell down
   d. showed signs of aging

9. Each year the local chiefs assembled all the underlined{eligible} young men.
   a. very intelligent
   c. suitable to be chosen
   b. physically strong
   d. belonging to a certain class

10. The Incas sent messages in *quipus*, which were colored strings with underlined{knots} in them.
    a. pieces tied together
    c. tiny, loose pieces
    b. long, separate pieces
    d. pieces hanging from something

WORDS THAT GO TOGETHER

A. *Find words in the reading that go together with the words below to make phrases.*

1. _____ intervals
2. majority _____
3. on _____ occasions
4. _____ exchange for
5. stood _____
6. _____ in the army
7. _____ control

B. *Complete the sentences with the phrases from Part A.*

1. When you give something in order to get something else in return, then you give one _____ the other.
2. _____ such as birthdays and weddings, we celebrate important events in our lives.

(continued)

3. People who are _____ of someone act according to certain rules and laws.

4. The _____ the people is most of the people.

5. You are _____ when you become a member of and spend time working in that part of a country's military.

6. Things that are _____ are spaced certain distances apart from each other.

7. If certain letters or objects represented something else, then they _____ that thing.

C. *Now use the phrases in your own sentences.*

EXAMPLE: *The traffic lights changed* at intervals *of two minutes.*

USE

Work with a partner to answer the questions. Use complete sentences.

1. What place was *abandoned* by early people who once lived there?

2. Where have you seen an object, group of letters, or a sign that *stood for* something else? What did it represent?

3. What are some of the characteristics of a *sophisticated* person?

4. In your country, what are the requirements to be *eligible* for marriage?

5. What do you wear *on special occasions* in your country? Talk about two different occasions.

6. What are two things that you are *allowed* to do when you reach a certain age in your family or in your country?

7. What are some things that occur *at intervals* of either time or space?

8. Why shouldn't you *neglect* your work or obligations?

COMPREHENSION

UNDERSTANDING MAIN IDEAS

Circle the letter of the best answer.

1. The main idea of paragraph 2 is that _____.
   a. the Incas allowed conquered people to keep their customs
   b. the first Incas lived in the Peruvian Andes in the 1100s

    c. Mayta Qapaq was a strong Inca leader

    d. a small tribe of Incas grew to a huge empire

2. The main idea of paragraph 5 is that _____.

    a. the Inca government had many officials

    b. the Sapa Inca was at the top of the pyramid

    c. Inca rule was very organized and controlled

    d. the farmers had many people telling them what to do

3. The main idea of paragraph 8 is that _____.

    a. the Inca roads would be hard to build today, even with modern tools

    b. the Inca road system was used mainly by soldiers

    c. most people were not allowed to travel in Inca society

    d. the Incas built a very advanced and complex system of roads

4. Paragraph 11 is mainly about how _____.

    a. the death of Huayna Capac led to war between his two sons

    b. the great Inca Empire was destroyed by the Spaniards

    c. the Spaniards were only interested in Inca gold and silver

    d. Atahualpa was not afraid of the Spaniards

REMEMBERING DETAILS

Reread the passage and fill in the blanks.

1. One Inca road, called the _____, was 3,250 miles (5,200 km) long.

2. For their first year of marriage, a couple did not have to pay _____.

3. In *quipus*, a yellow string stood for _____, a red string stood for _____, and the knots stood for _____.

4. Farmers had to send _____ to government storehouses.

5. The Spaniards promised Atahualpa his freedom in exchange for _____.

6. The Sapa Inca claimed to be _____.

(continued)

7. The job of the *chasquis* was to _____ to and from Cuzco.

8. The Incas had amazing suspension bridges made from

_____.

MAKING INFERENCES

The answers to these questions are not directly stated in the article. Write complete sentences.

1. What can you conclude about the Inca rulers from the statement that grain, gold, silver, cloth, and food poured into the capital from every part of the empire?

_____

2. What did the Incas probably believe about their dead rulers?

_____

3. What can be inferred about the Incas' attitude toward the elderly?

_____

4. What can you conclude about the lives of the ordinary people in the Inca Empire?

_____

5. Why do you suppose the Inca governors did not force their ideas on other groups?

_____

6. What do the Inca roads, buildings, and walls tell us about the Inca people?

_____

7. What terrible mistake did Atahualpa make?

_____

DISCUSSION

Discuss the answers to these questions with your classmates.

1. Why did the Spaniards so easily defeat the Incas? Do you think there was any possibility that the Incas could have won?

2. Why do you think the Incas abandoned Machu Picchu?

3. What are some of the good points about the Inca system of government? What are some of the bad points?

4. Were the Spaniards wise leaders like the Incas were when they conquered people? Explain your answer.

CRITICAL THINKING

Work with a partner. Ask each other the following questions. Discuss your answers.

1. What are some of the most ancient places in your country? Do you like to visit them? Why or why not? Does your government work to preserve historical places? Do you think it is important to study and preserve ancient sites around the world? Why or why not? What do we gain from the study of ancient civilizations?

2. What do you believe are the basic human rights that a country should grant its citizens? What are the basic responsibilities that citizens owe their country? How much control do you think a government should have over the lives of its citizens? What country or region do you believe has the most ideal form of government today? Explain.

WRITING

On separate paper, write a paragraph or an essay about one of the following topics.

1. What are two advantages and two disadvantages of living in an organized and controlled society, such as the society of the Incas?

2. Each country is different and has its own way of doing things. Write about two or three things that are done differently in another country.

3. Who should take care of the elderly? Write about the advantages and/or disadvantages of the government's taking care of the elderly.

GRAMMAR AND PUNCTUATION

COMMAS WITH TRANSITIONAL EXPRESSIONS: *HOWEVER, FOR EXAMPLE, THEREFORE, AS A MATTER OF FACT*

We use transitional expressions to act as a bridge between one sentence and another and between parts of a sentence. Transitional expressions can be used at the beginning, in the middle, or at the end of a sentence. We set them off with commas.

*For the first year, the couple did not pay taxes. **However,** they would have to work hard for the rest of their lives.*

*For the first year, the couple did not pay taxes. They would have to work hard, **however,** for the rest of their lives.*

(continued)

A. *Add commas to the following sentences where necessary.*

1. The Incas conquered many different peoples in South America. However they allowed them to keep their own customs.

2. There were huge storehouses all over the country. Therefore no one starved.

3. The roads were used by government messengers. The main reason for the roads however was for the soldiers to keep the empire under control.

4. The Royal Road is a great achievement. As a matter of fact it would be difficult to build even today.

5. The colors on the *quipus* represented what was being counted. Yellow for example stood for gold.

B. *Connect the two sentences with a transitional expression.*

1. The Spaniards were only interested in the gold and silver of the Incas. They made the people work in mines and neglect the farming.

   _____

   _____

2. Ordinary people had no freedom to go where they liked. They could not leave their village without permission.

   _____

   _____

Go to page 167 for the Internet Activity.

DID YOU KNOW?
- When an Inca died, his gold was not passed on to the next generation. Gold was buried with its owner.
- The Inca people had medicine for sadness, anger, cowardice, and fear, as well as for regular health problems.
- The Incas made highly-prized pots in the shape of peanuts.

HOW DO HINDUS CELEBRATE THE DIWALI FESTIVAL?

before you read

Answer these questions.

1. What is your favorite holiday? Why?
2. What special things do you do to celebrate the holiday?
3. How long do the celebrations last?

How Do Hindus Celebrate the Diwali Festival?

1   Diwali is the Hindu festival of light. The Hindus in India celebrate their favorite festival on the dark and cold nights of late October or early November. *Diwali*, which is **short for** *dipawali*, means "row of lights." There are lights everywhere during this festival, which is as important to Hindus as Christmas is to Christians. Houses have lights in front of their doors and windows, the streets are decorated with lights, and the temples have tiny **rows of** lights all over. Diwali, which lasts for five days, is one of the longest festivals for Hindus. In India, it's a time when everything stops. Families get together, eat together, and exchange gifts, usually of candies. They go shopping and buy things, from new clothes to new homes.

2   As with other Indian festivals, Diwali has a different **significance** for people in various parts of India, **depending upon** which gods the people worship at this time. However, the basic reason for this festival is the same all over India: Diwali is a time for new beginnings. It is a time when light **triumphs** over darkness and good triumphs over evil.

3   Before celebrating Diwali, Hindus prepare and decorate their homes. People **make sure that** their houses are **spotless**. Every house is repainted and **thoroughly** cleaned. They decorate the floors and sidewalks outside their homes with special *rangoli* patterns to welcome guests. *Rangoli* means "a mixture of colors." The patterns are created from a paste made from rice flour. The paste is usually colored red or yellow. The Hindus believe red and yellow make the evil spirits go away. One traditional Hindu pattern is the lotus flower, which is the symbol of one of their gods, Lakshmi.

4   Lights play an important part in the Diwali festival. Weeks before the festival, potters make clay lamps called *diwas*. On the first day of Diwali, every family buys a new lamp, which symbolizes new beginnings. There are lights everywhere in the streets, and thousands of these clay lamps can be seen. The lamps welcome travelers and help visitors find the houses they are going to visit. They are also there so the gods that people are remembering will see the lights and **pay** them **a visit**. In addition to light, there is noise—the noise of firecrackers. Families spend a lot of money on firecrackers and light them for four or five hours at night in their backyards and gardens. At the end of Diwali, there are big fireworks **displays** that light up the sky.

5   Hindus start every day of Diwali by taking a bath. After their baths, family members will rub scented oils into each other's hair. Then they get dressed in new clothes for the festival. Women will wear lots of jewelry and may draw special patterns on their hands and feet with *henna*. Then they pray at the family **shrine**.

Every Hindu home has a shrine with pictures and statues of different gods. The shrine is usually in the living room of the house, where it is easy to get together every day and pray. After people pray at the shrine, they go out and visit family, friends, and business **colleagues**. They take gifts of candies and dry fruits with them. They believe if you give sweet things, people will think sweet things about you. Some people may go to the market, where there are stalls selling sweets, flowers, and jewelry. There's also village dancing, and everyone can join in. At the end of the day, they all go home to eat and light fireworks.

6   Diwali is a time when people look forward to good luck and wealth in the year to come. The Hindu goddess of wealth, Lakshmi, is **honored** during the festival. People hope that a visit from this goddess will bring them good luck. To help Lakshmi enter their homes, they leave all the windows and doors open and make sure there are lights shining at every door and window so that she can find her way in easily. Businesspeople put out all their account books for Lakshmi to inspect. Hindus pay their bills and leave money and jewelry on the shrine to her in their houses.

7   In western India, Diwali starts the new business year. There is a ceremony of closing the account books and showing them to Lakshmi. Businesspeople who **take part in** the ceremony have red marks on their foreheads. During Diwali, people always visit their coworkers and send "Happy Diwali" cards and exchange gifts.

8   Hindus in other parts of the world also celebrate Diwali. Outside India, the temple is more important in the festivities than the home is. This is because Diwali is not a long public holiday in other countries, and Hindus have to go to work as usual. The temple is a good place for them to meet for the festivities. Outside India, Hindus usually spend their whole day in the temple, whereas in India they would go there to pray to the gods and then go home. In the temple during Diwali, priests dress the figures of the gods in brightly colored silk clothes to receive their visitors. When visitors come, they ring the temple bell to **let** the gods **know** that they have arrived, and they bring gifts of sweets and flowers. The temple is usually covered with offerings of sweets, flowers, fruit, and cakes. People bring food not only for the gods but also for themselves. Everybody eats and listens to traditional music. There are no **formal** religious services, but every visitor says a private prayer to the gods and asks for good fortune.

9   Diwali is a time to be happy and enjoy family and friends. It's a time when people exchange sweets, wear their new clothes, buy jewelry, and have a festive time. However, for the Hindus, Diwali is more than eating and shopping. Its burning lamp is a message of peace and **harmony** to the world.

VOCABULARY

MEANING

Circle the letter of the answer that is closest in meaning to the underlined word.

1. They <u>thoroughly</u> clean their houses.
   - **a.** partly
   - **b.** mostly
   - **c.** completely
   - **d.** generally

2. There are no <u>formal</u> religious services.
   - **a.** not like any other
   - **b.** official
   - **c.** taking a long time
   - **d.** taking place every day

3. In various parts of India, different gods are <u>honored</u>.
   - **a.** shown praise and respect
   - **b.** asked a favor of
   - **c.** given special names
   - **d.** talked about by everyone

4. The burning lamp is a message of peace and <u>harmony</u>.
   - **a.** acting according to reason
   - **b.** having a great love for other people
   - **c.** being quiet and restful
   - **d.** being in agreement with others

5. They pray at the family <u>shrine</u>.
   - **a.** a kind of ceremony
   - **b.** a place for worship
   - **c.** an area for entertainment
   - **d.** an important meal

6. They make sure their houses are <u>spotless</u>.
   - **a.** almost empty
   - **b.** very bright
   - **c.** like new
   - **d.** completely clean

7. It is a time when light <u>triumphs</u> over darkness.
   - **a.** tries to control
   - **b.** wins a victory
   - **c.** has a strong feeling against
   - **d.** makes better

8. They visit business <u>colleagues</u>.
   - **a.** people who work together
   - **b.** people who play on the same sports team
   - **c.** people who are wealthy
   - **d.** family members

9. Diwali has different <u>significance</u> for people in various parts of India.

    a. history and customs   **c.** importance and meaning

    b. type of ceremony   **d.** time and place

10. There are fireworks <u>displays</u> that light up the sky.

    a. shows that people see   **c.** noises that people hear

    b. songs that people sing   **d.** ceremonies that people take part in

WORDS THAT GO TOGETHER

A. *Find words in the reading that go together with the words below to make phrases.*

1. _____ . . . know
2. _____ . . . a visit
3. take part _____
4. rows _____
5. _____ sure that
6. depending _____
7. short _____

B. *Complete the sentences with the phrases from Part A.*

1. When you have _____ things, they are arranged side by side in a line.
2. When you _____ people _____, you go to see them and spend time with them.
3. If one thing may change because of something else, it is _____ something else.
4. If you _____ a person _____ about something, you tell them about it.
5. When you use part of a word instead of the whole word, then the smaller word is _____ the larger one.
6. When you _____ something happens, you do everything you can to be certain that it does happen.
7. When you do something with other people, you _____ that activity.

(continued)

C. *Now use the phrases in your own sentences.*

EXAMPLE: *I* let *my friend* know *about the free concert tickets.*

USE

Work with a partner to answer the questions. Use complete sentences.

1. What is the name of a famous *shrine*? Where is it? Why is it famous?
2. What is the *significance* of a white dress in your culture?
3. Where can you find *rows of* chairs?
4. Which people are *honored* in your country? Why are they honored?
5. If you could *pay* someone famous *a visit*, who would you choose to see?
6. In your culture, what type of clothing is *formal*?
7. What happens when people don't live in *harmony*?
8. What are some words that you use every day that are *short for* other words?

COMPREHENSION

UNDERSTANDING MAIN IDEAS

Some of the following statements are main ideas and some are supporting statements. Some of them are stated directly in the reading. Find the statements. Write M for each main idea. Write S for each supporting statement.

_____ 1. Diwali, which lasts for five days, is one of the longest festivals for Hindus.

_____ 2. Lights play an important part in the Diwali festival.

_____ 3. Diwali is a time when people look forward to good luck and wealth in the year to come.

_____ 4. Businesspeople who take part in the ceremony have red marks on their foreheads.

_____ 5. Hindus in other parts of the world also celebrate Diwali.

REMEMBERING DETAILS

Reread the passage and answer the questions. Write complete sentences.

1. How do Hindus start every day of Diwali?

   _____

2. What does *rangoli* mean?

   _____

3. During Diwali, what decorates the windows and doors of houses?

   _____

4. What do family members do after they pray at the shrine?

   _____

5. In the temple, how do priests dress the figures of the gods?

   _____

6. What colors do the Hindus believe make the evil spirits go away?

   _____

7. During Diwali, what does a new lamp symbolize?

   _____

8. Lakshmi is the goddess of what?

   _____

MAKING INFERENCES

The answers to these questions can be inferred, or guessed, from the reading. Circle the letter of the best answer.

1. The reading implies that the Diwali festival _____.
   a. is celebrated in the same way by all Hindus
   b. is a time for family and friends to get together
   c. makes many people wealthy
   d. is a good time for praying alone and having quiet thoughts

2. It can be inferred from the reading that the festival is celebrated with _____.
   a. a belief in the importance of the past
   b. a sense of sorrow for one's mistakes
   c. a spirit of hope for the future
   d. a joy in showing off one's wealth

3. From the reading, it can be concluded that Hindus _____.
   a. work hard to prepare for the festival
   b. don't believe in praying for good luck
   c. celebrate Diwali mostly in their homes
   d. dress very plainly during the festival

(continued)

4. The reading implies that Diwali is a time for _____.

    a. working hard at your job

    b. going to bed early and getting lots of rest

    c. staying home and praying

    d. doing good things for others

DISCUSSION

Discuss the answers to these questions with your classmates.

1. Why are holidays and festivals important to societies?

2. Many colors have special meanings or create certain feelings when we look at them. Name three colors and what they symbolize. What is your favorite color? Why?

3. All countries have their own customs. What is one custom that you like? What is one that you don't like? Explain your reasons.

CRITICAL THINKING

Work with a partner. Ask each other the following questions. Discuss your answers.

1. What does this sentence mean: "It is a time when light triumphs over darkness and good triumphs over evil"? Why is darkness associated with evil, and light associated with goodness? What are some other symbols of good and evil?

2. Holidays and festivals bring friends and family members together in common celebration. Why is this important to individuals and to society? What are some good things that happen at these times? What are some problems that can happen?

WRITING

On separate paper, write a paragraph or an essay about one of the following topics.

1. Write about your favorite holiday and how it is celebrated in your country.

2. Write about a festival you know that is celebrated differently in another country.

3. Write about two or three customs that you like. Give reasons why you like them.

GRAMMAR AND PUNCTUATION

DIRECT AND INDIRECT SPEECH

We use quotation marks for direct speech (a person's exact words). We use quotation marks at the beginning and at the end of each part of a direct quotation. We put punctuation inside the second pair of quotation marks. We do not use quotation marks for reported, or indirect, speech.

The woman said, "We must keep the tradition alive outside India." (direct speech)
"We must," the woman said, "keep the tradition alive outside India." (direct speech)
The woman said that they had to keep the tradition alive outside India. (indirect speech)

Write C for correct sentences. Rewrite the incorrect sentences with correct punctuation.

_____ 1. The woman said that "there were statues of different gods in the shrine."

_____

_____ 2. He told us that Hindus usually end their meal with *lassi*.

_____

_____ 3. The woman said, "Guests who visit between mealtimes receive special snacks."

_____

_____ 4. "The symbol of Lakshmi, she said, is a lotus flower."

_____

_____ 5. He said that today they are putting metal lamps on their shrines.

_____

_____ 6. Spices she said are the essence of Indian cuisine.

_____

Go to page 168 for the Internet Activity.

DID YOU KNOW?

- For Diwali, people whitewash their houses and buy new household items such as utensils. In recent years they are also buying electronic equipment and even cars!
- According to one belief, the sound of firecrackers shows the joy of people living on earth, making the gods aware of their state.
- There is a tradition of gambling during Diwali. It is believed that the Goddess Parvarti gambled with her husband and said whoever gambled during Diwali would prosper in the coming year.

WHAT IS THE STORY BEHIND THE 1,001 ARABIAN NIGHTS?

before you read

Answer these questions.

1. What kinds of stories do you like? Adventure? Mystery? Romance?
2. What are some famous stories or folktales?
3. Which stories are popular in your country?

What Is the Story Behind The 1,001 Arabian Nights?

1   *The 1,001 Arabian Nights*, also known as *The Book of One Thousand and One Nights*, is one of the most famous pieces of Arabic literature. It includes many well-known stories, such as "Ali Baba and the Forty Thieves," "Sinbad the Sailor," and "Aladdin's Lamp." In all, the collection of stories contains about 200 folktales from Arabia, India, Persia (modern day Iran), and even China. Many people in these countries shared a religion—Islam—and the Arabic language of the Koran.

2   These stories are very ancient and are believed to have first been told by an Arab storyteller in the ninth century. There are various types of stories: love stories, historical tales, comedies, tragedies, and religious legends. The stories **depict** what life was like at the time and include good and bad rulers, magicians, and lots of adventure. The stories have been told and retold for generations. Later on in the Middle Ages, a "frame" to all these stories was added. The frame for the large group of stories is the story of Scheherazade. In her tale, she tells many of *The 1,001 Arabian Nights* stories.

3   The story of Scheherazade begins with the tale of a king named Shahryar who rules an unnamed island "between India and China." Shahryar had a wife whom he loved more than anything in the world. He was **devoted to** her and would do anything for her. However, after several years, he discovered that she had been **unfaithful** to him. **Betrayed**, the king **carried out** the law of the land and ordered his chief minister to put her to death. Then the heartbroken king **went out of his mind** and declared that all women were unfaithful like his wife. The fewer there were of them, he thought, the better the world would be. So every evening he married a new wife and commanded that she be **executed** the following morning.

4   It was the job of the chief minister to provide the king with these unfortunate brides. The chief minister did his duty with great **reluctance**, for it was hard for him to see a woman married one day and then killed the next. The people of the town lived in sadness and fear. Fathers and mothers cried about the fate of their daughters. The chief minister himself had two daughters: Scheherazade and Dinarzade. Scheherazade was older; she was a clever and brave girl. Her father had given her the best education, and she was one of the most beautiful girls in the kingdom.

5   One day, Scheherazade asked her father a favor. Her father loved her very much, and he would not refuse her anything that was reasonable. Scheherazade then told him that she was determined to end the cruel practice of the king. She had a plan to save the women of the kingdom from their terrible fate. Since her father had to

(continued)

provide the king with a new wife every day, she **implored** him to choose her. Her father was shocked by her request and thought she had **lost her senses**. But Scheherazade explained that if her plan succeeded, she would **do a** great **service for** her country. After she begged and begged him, her father finally agreed to Scheherazade's wish. He went to the palace to tell the king that the following evening he would bring him Scheherazade to be the new queen. The **astonished** king asked him why he would sacrifice his own daughter. The chief minister replied that it was her wish. The king then told the minister to bring his daughter to the palace.

6   When her father returned to tell her, Scheherazade was happy and thanked her father for agreeing to her wish. She then went to prepare herself for the marriage. But, first, she wanted to speak with her sister, Dinarzade. Scheherazade told her sister that she had a plan and needed her help. She said her father was going to take her to the palace to celebrate her marriage with the king. As a final wish, she would ask the king to let her sister sleep in their bedroom during the last night that she was alive. If the king **granted** her wish, which she hoped he would, then Dinarzade should wake her up an hour before daybreak and say these words to her: "My sister, if you are not asleep, please tell me one of your charming stories." Then Scheherazade would begin to tell a tale, and she hoped by this to save the people from their terrible fate. Dinarzade said she would do what her sister asked of her.

7   When the time for the marriage came, the chief minister took Scheherazade to the palace and left her alone with the king. The king told her to raise her veil and was amazed at her beauty. But Scheherazade had tears in her eyes. When the king asked what was the matter, Scheherazade said that she had a sister whom she loved very much, and she asked the king if he would allow her sister to spend the night in the same room since it would be the last time they would be together. The king agreed to her wish.

8   An hour before daybreak, Dinarzade woke up and asked Scheherazade for a story, adding, "It is the last time I'll have the pleasure of hearing you." Scheherazade asked the king if he would let her do as her sister requested. "Of course," answered the king. So Scheherazade began to tell the king a story. But when she reached the most exciting part of it, she stopped. She said that if he wanted to hear the end he would have to let her live another day. Each night she would tell him a story, ending at daybreak with a "cliffhanger," stopping at an exciting point.

9   The enchanted king always wanted to hear the rest of the story, and so he **put off** her death night after night. He was **dazzled** by her thrilling stories, and soon he fell in love with her. Scheherazade was able to **spin a** new **tale** each night for 1,001 nights. By this time, she had given birth to three sons, and the king became convinced of her faithfulness. Scheherazade's plan was successful, and all the people **rejoiced** because the women in the kingdom were saved.

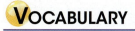

VOCABULARY

MEANING

Circle the letter of the answer that is closest in meaning to the underlined word.

1. The chief minister did his duty with great <u>reluctance</u>.
   - **a.** fear
   - **b.** unwillingness
   - **c.** eagerness
   - **d.** carelessness

2. Scheherazade <u>implored</u> her father to choose her.
   - **a.** begged
   - **b.** helped
   - **c.** screamed at
   - **d.** refused

3. The people <u>rejoiced</u> because the women were saved.
   - **a.** celebrated
   - **b.** relaxed
   - **c.** complained
   - **d.** laughed

4. The stories <u>depict</u> what life was like at the time.
   - **a.** create
   - **b.** copy
   - **c.** show
   - **d.** question

5. The king's wife was <u>unfaithful</u>.
   - **a.** jealous of him
   - **b.** untrue to him
   - **c.** confused by him
   - **d.** honest with him

6. The king was <u>dazzled</u> by Scheherazade's stories.
   - **a.** tired
   - **b.** angered
   - **c.** confused
   - **d.** amazed

7. The king commanded that every new wife be <u>executed</u> in the morning.
   - **a.** punished
   - **b.** beaten
   - **c.** killed
   - **d.** sent away

8. The <u>astonished</u> king asked Scheherazade's father why he would sacrifice his daughter.
   - **a.** angry
   - **b.** worried
   - **c.** surprised
   - **d.** eager

(continued)

9. The king <u>granted</u> Scheherazade's wish.

    a. refused   **c.** understood

    b. allowed   **d.** returned

10. The king was <u>betrayed</u> by his wife.

    a. warned   **c.** treated dishonestly

    b. controlled   **d.** not taken care of

WORDS THAT GO TOGETHER

A. *Find words in the reading that go together with the words below to make phrases.*

1. went out of his _____

2. _____ a service _____

3. carried _____

4. spin a _____

5. _____ her senses

6. devoted _____

7. _____ off

B. *Complete the sentences with the phrases from Part A.*

1. A person who makes up stories knows how to _____.

2. When something is accomplished or a rule is followed, it is

    _____.

3. If a man was so upset that he acted unreasonably, you might say that he

    _____.

4. When you _____ something, you delay it or make it wait

    until a later time.

5. If you are _____ someone or something, it means that you

    love and give great importance to that person or thing.

6. When you help people, you _____ them.

7. If a woman did something crazy and unusual, her friends might think that she had

    _____.

C. *Now use the phrases in your own sentences.*

EXAMPLE: *The manager watched his workers to make sure they* carried out *his requests.*

USE

Work with a partner to answer the questions. Use complete sentences.

1. Besides folktales, what else might *depict* what life was like in the past?
2. Has anyone ever *granted* a wish for you? What was your wish?
3. What are two historical events that *astonished* you?
4. What career would be good for someone who can *spin a tale*?
5. Have you experienced a situation where people *rejoiced*? What were some of the things they did to celebrate?
6. Who is a famous person in history who was *betrayed*?
7. Where might you be *dazzled* by what you see or hear?
8. Would you like to *do a service for* your country? What type of service?

COMPREHENSION

UNDERSTANDING MAIN IDEAS

Circle the letter of the best answer.

1. The main idea of paragraph 2 is that _____.
   a. the frame for many of the tales is the story of Scheherazade
   b. the stories were told in the ninth century
   c. the book is made up of many ancient stories
   d. the tales tell us about the past

2. The main idea of paragraph 5 is that _____.
   a. Scheherazade's father loved her very much
   b. Scheherazade wanted to marry the king in order to help her country
   c. both the king and Scheherazade's father were shocked by her wish to marry
   d. Scheherazade had to beg her father to let her marry the king

3. Paragraph 6 is mainly about Scheherazade's _____.
   a. happiness over her father's decision
   b. wish to have her sister with her
   c. marriage to the king
   d. plan to save the women

(continued)

4. The main idea of paragraph 8 is that _____.

    a. Scheherazade used stories to keep the king from executing her

    b. Dinarzade helped to save Scheherazade's life

    c. Scheherazade ended her story every night

    d. the king was kind to Scheherazade and her sister, Dinarzade

REMEMBERING DETAILS

Reread the passage and fill in the blanks.

1. The stories in *The 1,001 Arabian Nights* are from many countries, including
   _____, _____, _____, and _____.

2. The various kinds of stories in the book are _____, _____,
   _____, _____, and _____.

3. The king believed that all women were _____.

4. It was the job of the chief minister to provide the king with _____.

5. When the king raised Scheherazade's veil, he was amazed by _____.

6. As Scheherazade's last wish, she asked the king to _____.

7. In the morning, Dinarzade asked Scheherazade to _____.

8. The king put off Scheherazade's death night after night because _____.

MAKING INFERENCES

*Some of the following statements are facts from the reading. Other statements can be inferred, or guessed. Write **F** for each factual statement. Write **I** for each inference.*

_____ 1. *The 1,001 Arabian Nights* is one of the most famous books in Arabic literature.

_____ 2. The stories have been passed down through many generations.

_____ 3. The people of early times loved adventure stories just as people do today.

_____ 4. After the king learned of his wife's unfaithfulness, he was afraid to ever love another woman.

_____ 5. The townspeople cried because their daughters were being executed.

_____ 6. It was a great act of courage for Scheherazade to marry the king.

_____ 7. Scheherazade's father would not refuse any reasonable wish of hers.

_____ 8. Dinarzade was a loving and faithful sister.

_____ 9. Scheherazade was intelligent and understood human nature.

_____ 10. The people were overjoyed when the king fell in love with Scheherazade.

DISCUSSION

Discuss the answers to these questions with your classmates.

1. Why has storytelling always been important to people and societies? How were stories passed down in ancient times? How are they told today?

2. What are the qualities of a hero? What qualities did Scheherazade possess?

3. Sometimes friends or coworkers can betray each other, too. Describe this type of betrayal. What problems can it cause?

CRITICAL THINKING

Work with a partner. Ask each other the following questions. Discuss your answers.

1. In what ways does unfaithfulness hurt others? Can an unfaithful spouse change his or her ways? Why or why not? What happens to a person who has been betrayed by another? What problems does it cause this person in his or her life and relationships?

2. What are the purposes of storytelling? Is there still a place for storytelling in modern society? Why or why not?

WRITING

On separate paper, write a paragraph or an essay about one of the following topics.

1. Describe a famous folktale or story that you know.

2. Who do you think has the qualities of a hero? The person can be living or dead. Give reasons.

GRAMMAR AND PUNCTUATION

PARTICIPIAL ADJECTIVES

Participial adjectives are formed from the present and past participles of verbs. We use participles of verbs as adjectives: *charming / charmed; thrilling / thrilled; astonishing / astonished.*

1. The present participle acts as an adjective with an active meaning. These adjectives end in *-ing* and describe someone or something that <u>causes</u> a feeling or reaction.
   Please tell me one of your **charming** *stories before the sun rises.*

(continued)

2. The past participle acts as an adjective with a passive meaning. These adjectives end in
-*ed* and describe someone or something that experiences a feeling or reaction.
Dinarzade was **charmed** *by the stories.*

*Complete the sentences. Use participial adjectives formed by adding -ing or -ed to the verbs in
parentheses. Be careful! Sometimes there are spelling changes to the verb when we form
participial adjectives.*

1. The king looked forward to her _____ stories. (thrill)
2. The _____ king wanted to hear the end of the story. (dazzle)
3. Scheherazade stopped at the most _____ part of the story. (excite)
4. The daughters in the town were _____. (frighten)
5. Scheherazade's father was _____ to hear the news that his daughter wanted
   to marry the king. (shock)
6. The king was _____ that his minister would sacrifice his own daughter.
   (surprise)
7. There are many _____ stories in *The 1,001 Arabian Nights*. (amuse)
8. The story of "Sinbad the Sailor" is _____. (enchant)
9. King Shahryar was _____ to his wife. (devote)
10. The king thought Scheherazade's beauty was _____. (amaze)

Go to page 168 for the Internet Activity.

DID YOU KNOW?	• The stories of Aladdin's Lamp, Ali Baba and the Forty Thieves, and the Seven Voyages of Sinbad were Middle-eastern folktales. They were not in the original Arabic *Nights*. They were later put into the collection by European translators. • In 1980–1 explorer Tim Severin led an expedition from Oman to China, recreating the voyages of Sinbad the sailor. The government of Oman paid for the project.	

WHAT IS ANGKOR WAT?

before

you read

Answer these questions.

1. What are some famous religious buildings around the world?
2. What is the largest building in your country?
3. What are some of the most famous historical places around the world?

WHAT IS ANGKOR WAT?

1   Angkor Wat is the biggest religious building in the world. It is bigger than any other temple in Asia, the Great Pyramid in Egypt, or St. Peter's in Rome, and it is only one of a thousand temples in the Angkor region. Its design is so remarkable that some people regard it as one of the Seven Wonders of the World. Angkor Wat is located in present-day Cambodia, in Southeast Asia.

2   Angkor was long covered by **dense** jungle and was a forgotten place for many centuries. Wandering Buddhist monks sometimes passed by the temples on their way through the jungle. They didn't know how these magnificent temples had been built, so they **made up** stories about them. They said the temples had been built by gods in an ancient time. Some people said they had been built by giants. These legends eventually reached other places. Some Asians went in search of this mysterious city of the gods. Eventually some European adventurers heard the stories about the lost city of the jungle, but most people didn't believe them.

3   In 1860, Henri Mahout, a Frenchman, became the first European to see Angkor. Mahout was in the Cambodian jungle looking for plant species that were unknown in France. Soon, local people told him about "temples built by giants in the jungle." Mahout was curious, so he hired local guides and started to look for the temples. Other explorers before him had searched but had never found anything. Mahout was lucky. He found the city and its magnificent temple. He spent three weeks drawing the temple. It is now called Angkor Wat, which means "city temple." We do not know what its builders called it. Unfortunately, Mahout died of fever in the jungle at age 35. His **diaries** and drawings were taken to France where people began to be curious about this place. Soon visitors came to see it. Among them was Anna Leonowens, the British governess to the king of Siam. Her life story later became the **feature of** the musical, *The King and I*. Other people came to steal **artifacts**. Historians and archeologists came to find out more about this ancient city and its temples. They still continue to do so today.

4   The archeologists and historians were lucky because the walls of the temple were covered with **inscriptions** to tell us the story. These inscriptions were written in Sanskrit, an ancient language that greatly influenced Cambodian. They tell us that the builders of Angkor Wat were the **ancestors** of today's Cambodians. One thousand years ago, Angkor was the capital of an empire that covered parts of present-day Thailand, Cambodia, Laos, and Vietnam. About a million people lived in the city of Angkor at one time. The city was founded in the ninth century and was **abandoned** by the fifteenth.

5   Angkor Wat was built in the twelfth century **at the peak of** the empire's wealth and power. It was built for King Suryavarman II as his royal temple and **dedicated to** the Hindu gods. The temple includes a series of towers, the highest of which is 213 feet (65 meters) high. It is the largest and most beautiful temple of all the

buildings of Angkor. It is built in the style of Khmer architecture. It was made of sandstone blocks that were carried about 23 miles (40 km) to the site. The stones were fitted together with extreme **accuracy** and skill, with no cement being used. For example, there is a 660-foot-long (201 meters) corridor with measurements accurate to a **fraction** of an inch. The building took 37 years to build, but one modern engineer has said that it would take 300 years to build Angkor Wat today. All of its surfaces have carvings that show gods, men, and animals, as well as armies and battles. The walls also tell us about the lives of the ancient people of Angkor. They grew rice and fished. They needed a lot of rice for the 1 million residents of the city and for the empire's armies. They grew rice by making a system of waterways for their huge rice fields.

6   We do not know why Angkor was deserted. Some people think there was a **famine**. Some say that the Khmer people were so **distracted** with building that their enemies came and took over the city. Whatever the reason, around 1430, the Thai people attacked Angkor and took away its people as slaves.

7   The city was abandoned, but the temple remained. Although originally built as a Hindu temple, it later became a Buddhist temple. For 400 years, Buddhist monks lived there and stopped the jungle from taking over the temple. Although they cleared the thick brush around the roofs, walls, and courtyards, they could not take away the trees that were centuries old. To this day the trees' enormous roots and trunks are breaking apart the ancient stones.

8   In the 1990s, art historian Dr. Eleanor Mannikka looked into the mysteries of Angkor Wat. She measured the temple's structure **in detail** and used the same unit of measure as the Khmer builders, which was the *hat*. This equaled the distance from a person's elbow to the tip of the middle finger. According to Mannikka, the measurements formed a code recording the cycles of the sun and moon and important dates in the history of the Khmer. She also noticed that the temple was designed so as to **make use of** the sun's rays falling on important carvings. The sun's rays would fall on an important carving on important religious days. Mannikka believes that the designs of the temple were very special and were meant to protect its people, although many specialists do not believe her theories. There are other theories, too. Perhaps one day we will know.

9   Today Angkor Wat has become a symbol of Cambodia. It is rare for a flag to have **an image of** a building, but Angkor Wat appears on Cambodia's national flag. It is also the main attraction for tourists visiting the country. Angkor Wat was declared a World Heritage Site by UNESCO in 1992, which means that it has outstanding cultural or natural importance to the entire world and that it should be protected for all time.

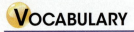

VOCABULARY

MEANING

Circle the letter of the answer that is closest in meaning to the underlined word.

1. Angkor Wat was covered by <u>dense</u> jungle.
   a. dark
   b. thick
   c. tall
   d. old

2. His <u>diaries</u> and drawings were taken to France.
   a. records of a person's life
   b. writings about the history of places
   c. stories about things that did not really happen
   d. poems about great heroes

3. Other people came to steal <u>artifacts</u>.
   a. writings left by others who came before
   b. remains of plants and animals from long ago
   c. objects made by humans in an earlier time
   d. anything in nature, either present or past

4. The walls of the temple were covered with <u>inscriptions</u>.
   a. objects that tell a story
   b. pictures made on cloth
   c. writings made on a surface
   d. marks left by nature

5. The builders of Angkor Wat were the <u>ancestors</u> of today's Cambodians.
   a. family members, such as aunts and uncles
   b. citizens of the same country
   c. people who live far away
   d. relatives who lived long ago

6. The city was founded in the ninth century and <u>abandoned</u> by the fifteenth.

    a. left completely

    b. passed by

    c. filled up

    d. made famous

7. The stones were fitted together with extreme <u>accuracy</u>.

    a. exactly correct

    b. in a unique way

    c. with some errors

    d. in a normal way

8. The measurements were accurate to a <u>fraction</u> of an inch.

    a. a complete whole

    b. almost an entire piece

    c. a very small part

    d. a combination of two things

9. Some people think there was a <u>famine</u>.

    a. a time when there are floods

    b. a time when there is no rain

    c. a time when there is no leadership

    d. a time when there is no food

10. Some say that the Khmer people were so <u>distracted</u> that their enemies took over the city.

    a. thinking about what one is doing

    b. thinking about the future

    c. thinking about what is important

    d. thinking about something else

WORDS THAT GO TOGETHER

A. *Find words in the reading that go together with the words below to make phrases.*

1. feature _____

2. dedicated _____

3. _____ use _____

4. at _____ peak _____

5. made _____

6. _____ image _____

7. _____ detail

B. *Complete the sentences with the phrases from Part A.*

1. Something you created or invented is something you _____.

2. When you employ something for a purpose you _____ it.

3. The _____ your party, show, or event would be the most special part of it.

4. If you looked at every single part of something, you looked at it _____.

5. When something is done for a cause, purpose, or person, it is _____ it.

6. To be _____ something means to be at the highest point or level.

7. _____ something is a picture of it or an object made to represent it.

C. *Now use the phrases in your own sentences.*

EXAMPLE: *The artist was* at the peak of *her career.*

USE

Work with a partner to answer the questions. Use complete sentences.

1. What can be one of the reasons for a *famine*?

2. What are you able to accomplish with *accuracy*?

3. What are some places in the world that have *dense* forests?

4. What kinds of things do people write in a *diary*?

5. What do you have that once belonged to your *ancestors*?

6. What is a kind of *artifact* that we see in museums?

7. What is another ancient place where *inscriptions* have been found?

8. What is something that makes you *distracted* when you are trying to do work?

COMPREHENSION

UNDERSTANDING MAIN IDEAS

Circle the letter of the best answer.

1. Paragraph 2 is mainly about _____.
   a. where Angkor Wat was built
   b. the legends about Angkor Wat
   c. who went in search of Angkor Wat
   d. the Buddhist monks who passed by Angkor Wat

2. The main idea of paragraph 3 is that _____.
   a. local people believed Angkor Wat had been built by giants
   b. many explorers tried to find Angkor Wat
   c. a famous woman went to see Angkor Wat
   d. Henry Mahout found Angkor Wat and left records of it

3. The main idea of paragraph 5 is that Angkor Wat was _____.
   a. dedicated to the Hindu gods
   b. made with sandstone blocks accurately put together
   c. covered with beautiful stone carvings
   d. an amazing structure built with great skill

4. Paragraph 8 is mainly about Dr. Eleanor Mannikka's _____.
   a. detailed measurements of the temple
   b. knowledge of the history of the Khmer people
   c. theories about the design of the temple
   d. study of important carvings

REMEMBERING DETAILS

Reread the passage and circle the letter of the best answer.

1. Wandering Buddhist monks _____.
   - **a.** helped to build Angkor Wat
   - **b.** knew who built Angkor Wat
   - **c.** created stories about Angkor Wat
   - **d.** forgot about Angkor Wat

2. *Angkor Wat* means _____.
   - **a.** temple built by giants
   - **b.** temple in the jungle
   - **c.** city temple
   - **d.** hidden temple

3. Henri Mahout found Angkor Wat _____.
   - **a.** with the help of local people
   - **b.** while he was looking for another place
   - **c.** after other explorers told him where it was
   - **d.** after searching for three weeks

4. In the fifteenth century, Angkor Wat _____.
   - **a.** was in the process of being built
   - **b.** had a population of 1 million people
   - **c.** was at its height of success
   - **d.** was already empty of people

5. The temple of Angkor Wat is built with a series of _____.
   - **a.** stone blocks
   - **b.** towers
   - **c.** circles
   - **d.** Hindu gods

6. From the wall writings, we know the Khmer people _____.
   - **a.** suffered from a lack of food
   - **b.** grew rice and fished
   - **c.** didn't know how to measure accurately
   - **d.** had very little water

7. While Buddhist monks lived at Angkor Wat, they _____.
   - **a.** allowed the temple to be taken over the by jungle
   - **b.** built new roofs, walls, and courtyards
   - **c.** planted new trees
   - **d.** protected the temple from the jungle

8. Dr. Mannikka believed the Khmer made use of the sun's rays to _____.
   - **a.** shine light on important carvings
   - **b.** record the cycles of the moon
   - **c.** protect the people
   - **d.** create a unit of measurement

MAKING INFERENCES

The answers to these questions are not directly stated in the article. Write complete sentences.

1. What can be inferred about the monks who said the temples had been built by the gods?
2. What did Mahout's diaries and drawings do for other adventurers?
3. What can you infer from the statement that "the archeologists and historians were lucky because the walls of the temple were covered with inscriptions"?
4. What can you conclude about the builders of Angkor Wat?
5. From the carvings on the walls, what can you conclude about the religious beliefs of the Khmer people?
6. What can you infer about the Buddhist monks who lived in Angkor Wat?
7. What can you infer from the statement "There are other theories, too"?
8. How do you suppose the people of Cambodia feel about Angkor Wat?

DISCUSSION

Discuss the answers to these questions with your classmates.

1. What are some places in your country that have historical importance? What is being done to protect them? Do you like to visit historical places? Why or why not?
2. What are some places in the world that have engineering wonders of both ancient and modern times? Are any of these places in your country?
3. Who were the earliest people to live in your country? What was their religion? Where did they live? What were their houses like? What did they wear and eat? Were they farmers, nomads, or merchants? Do you have an interest in learning about your family's ancestors? Why or why not?
4. Many people have stolen artifacts from Angkor Wat and other historical places around the world. Why do people steal artifacts? Who helps to create a market for them? How can the theft of artifacts be prevented?

CRITICAL THINKING

Work with a partner. Ask each other the following questions. Discuss your answers.

1. Mahout died of fever in the jungle. Many explorers died during their expeditions. Why do you think people have always wanted to explore other places? What

(continued)

characteristics do explorers have? Why do they risk their lives trying to find places where no one else has gone before? What hardships do you think Mahout experienced in the jungle? What are the advantages and disadvantages of being an explorer? Do you like to travel and explore places you have never seen? Why or why not?

2. So many tourists visit Angkor Wat that it is suffering new damage. How can tourists help to protect culturally important places? What are some ways in which governments, organizations, and individuals can each contribute to the protection of important historical or natural places? Do you think the problem should be a global effort, or should it be the responsibility of the local government? Explain.

WRITING

On separate paper, write a paragraph or an essay about one of the following topics.

1. Write a biography of a famous explorer
2. Write an argument for or against this idea: Artifacts in famous museums stolen from historical sites should be returned to where they came from.

GRAMMAR AND PUNCTUATION

SEMICOLONS

1. When there is no coordinating conjunction (*and, but, or, for, nor, so, yet*) between independent clauses in a sentence and the relationship is clear, we use a semicolon (;) to separate them.
   The city was founded in the ninth century; it was abandoned by the fifteenth.

2. If the relationship between the independent clauses is not clear with a semicolon alone, we can use a transitional expression as well.
   The temple was built as a Hindu temple; however, it later became a Buddhist temple.

Add semicolons to the following sentences where necessary.

1. Some people came to see it because they were curious others came to steal artifacts.
2. Historians were lucky the walls of the temple were covered with inscriptions.
3. The carvings show gods, men and animals, and battles in addition, they tell us about the lives of the people.
4. Her theory was that the temple was designed to protect its people however, others do not believe this theory.

5. The city was founded in the ninth century it was abandoned by the fifteenth.

6. A lot of rice was grown therefore, a system of waterways was developed for their rice fields.

7. Angkor was the capital of an empire about a million people lived there at one time.

8. The monks cleared the thick brush as much as they could they could not take away the trees that were centuries old.

9. The temple is 213 feet (65 meters) high it is the largest and most beautiful temple of all the buildings of Angkor.

10. Mahout wanted others to believe what he had discovered he made detailed descriptions and drawings of his find.

Go to page 169 for the Internet Activity.

DID YOU KNOW?

- The Khmer, a Hindu people, built their wealth on rice.
- About 90 percent of Cambodians today are of Khmer descent, and Angkor Wat has become a symbol of their ancient culture.
- Over a million tourists visit Angkor Wat each year.

WHAT DOES HAIR TELL US ABOUT PEOPLE?

before you read

Answer these questions.

1. Do you like your current hairstyle? Why or why not?
2. What does a hairstyle say about a person?
3. If you could have any hairstyle, what would it be?

WHAT DOES HAIR TELL US ABOUT PEOPLE?

1   Throughout history, hair has always been used to **make a fashion statement**. It also tells us a lot about culture. In almost all societies, people have cut or styled their hair for practical or decorative reasons. For example, the ancient Greeks liked blond hair, so both men and women lightened their hair. On the other hand, the Romans preferred dark hair. The Assyrian culture made an art of hairstyling. People curled, oiled, and perfumed their hair; they also cut their hair and beards in **layers**. Assyrian soldiers needed to have their hair properly curled before they went to war. The Assyrian people used hairstyles to show their position and occupation. Assyrian women of high rank, as well as women in Egypt, put on **fake** beards at meetings to show authority.

2   Hair is often a sign of superiority. Primitive men put bones, feathers, and other objects in their hair to impress and **intimidate** their enemies. Later, the Romans made the people they conquered cut off their hair to show submission. In seventeenth-century China, men shaved the front of the hair and combed the hair in the back into a braided tail. They also made those they conquered wear this style.

3   Some cultures consider hair to be a **sensuous** object. For some people, not having hair or not showing it to others is a sign of religious devotion. Christian and Buddhist monks often shave their heads to show holiness and retirement from the world. Many Christian nuns cover their hair. Some Muslim women cover their hair when they are **in public**, and men in certain countries wear a turban or head cloth for religious reasons.

4   In ancient and modern times, hair has been used to **reveal** a person's emotions, **marital status**, or age. For example, ancient Egyptian men and women usually shaved their hair. However, when they were **in mourning**, they grew it long. Hindu women, on the other hand, cut off their long hair as a sign of mourning. In medieval Europe, unmarried women showed their long hair in public, whereas married women covered theirs. Today, brides in the Maasai tribe in Africa have their heads shaved as part of their marriage ceremony, and mothers in the tribe shave their sons' hair when the boys become adolescents. Today, teenagers all over the world **demonstrate** their youth and individuality through haircuts or hair colors. Even in countries like China and Japan, where dyed hair is considered untraditional, up to 68 percent of women and 20 percent of men—most of them young—now use hair color to **reflect** their individual personalities.

5   Wigs have always been popular as fashion statements and as signs of wealth or status. Ancient Egyptians shaved their heads for cleanliness and then covered their

(continued)

heads with wigs. The higher the status of a person, the bigger his or her wig was. Cleopatra wore different styles and colors of wigs, and another Egyptian queen wore such a heavy wig on important occasions that attendants had to help her walk. Queen Elizabeth I of England wore a red wig because her own red hair was falling out, so all the rich men and women copied her and either dyed their hair red or wore red wigs. In France, King Louis XIV, who was also going bald, started the fashion of elaborate wigs. Naturally, everyone wanted to look like him, so they all started to wear wigs, too. At one time, forty wig makers were employed full-time just to make wigs for the people in the palace of Versailles!

6   These elaborate wig fashions went over to England, which always copied the French for style. Wigs became common for the middle and upper classes in England and France. They were powdered white because people thought this **flattered** the face and made their eyes look brighter. The fashion spread to divisions of the law, the army, and the navy, each of which had its own style of wig. However, by the end of the 1700s, hairstyles for women became extravagant to the point of **ridicule**. Rich women would spend hours with hairdressers who built tall wire cages on the women's heads. They covered the cages with hair and wigs and then greased the hair with fat so the white powder would stick to it. Finally, they decorated the hair with jewels, feathers, ornaments, and even flowers with water containers to keep them fresh. The women would wear their hair this way for two or three weeks. Obviously, they had to sleep in a sitting position at night, and they could not wash their hair, but once a week they had to "open the hair" to get rid of the insects living in it. Fortunately, the French Revolution in 1789 put an end to such extravagance, and hairstyles became simple again.

7   In the twentieth century, women in Western cultures used their hair to show their growing independence. They often simplified their hairstyles to fit their busy lifestyles. For example, in the 1920s and 1930s, women cut their hair as **a symbol of** liberation. In the 1950s and 1960s, many women in the United States used wigs to **save time**. Instead of styling their hair every morning, they would wear a prestyled wig. Some women alternated between several wigs so that they could choose a style or color to match their clothes or even their mood!

8   Due to such changes, fashionable hairstyles no longer were **limited to** the rich—they were for everyone. As the popularity of movies and television grew, women started to copy the hairstyles of famous stars, such as the short cut of Greta Garbo or the platinum blond hair color of Jean Harlow. More recently, thousands of American women **imitated** Jennifer Aniston's "Rachel" haircut seen on the popular TV show *Friends*. Men and boys also copy the hairstyles of movie or sports stars. In England, for example, boys often have their hair cut like the British soccer player David Beckham.

9   Today's hairstyles have become more relaxed and individual, so both men and women can choose a style that fits their lives and expresses their personalities. Whether they are rich or poor, people can choose the color or style of their hair—or even of a wig—to suit their own tastes.

VOCABULARY

MEANING

Circle the letter of the answer that is closest in meaning to the underlined word.

1. Assyrians cut their hair in <u>layers</u>.
   - **a.** unusual shapes
   - **b.** different levels
   - **c.** special ceremonies
   - **d.** short styles

2. Today, teenagers <u>demonstrate</u> their youth and individuality through haircuts or hair colors.
   - **a.** celebrate
   - **b.** hide
   - **c.** behave like
   - **d.** show

3. Women <u>imitated</u> the haircut seen on a popular TV show.
   - **a.** laughed at
   - **b.** did the opposite of
   - **c.** took parts of
   - **d.** did the same as

4. Women in Egypt put on <u>fake</u> beards.
   - **a.** not real
   - **b.** colorful
   - **c.** newly made
   - **d.** natural

5. Hairstyles for women became extravagant to the point of <u>ridicule</u>.
   - **a.** being made fun of
   - **b.** getting respect for
   - **c.** being famous for
   - **d.** receiving praise for

6. Both women and men now use hair color to <u>reflect</u> their personalities.
   - **a.** try to hide
   - **b.** give a sign of
   - **c.** try to change
   - **d.** make better

7. Some cultures consider hair to be a <u>sensuous</u> object.
   - **a.** having a certain style
   - **b.** pleasing to the senses
   - **c.** looking very unusual
   - **d.** making a lot of trouble

8. Wigs were powdered white because people thought this <u>flattered</u> the face.
   - **a.** made it smaller
   - **b.** made it more pale
   - **c.** made it more attractive
   - **d.** made it look younger

(continued)

9. Primitive men put objects in their hair to <u>intimidate</u> their enemies.

    a. kill   **c.** defeat

    b. harm   **d.** frighten

10. Hair has been used to <u>reveal</u> a person's emotions, marital status, or age.

    a. try to cover   **c.** make known

    b. show respect for   **d.** laugh at

WORDS THAT GO TOGETHER

A. *Find words in the reading that go together with the words below to make phrases.*

1. limited _____

2. _____ public

3. _____ symbol _____

4. _____ mourning

5. marital _____

6. _____ a _____ statement

7. _____ time

B. *Complete the sentences with the phrases from Part A.*

1. When you are _____, you feel very sad because someone special to you has died.

2. To do something more quickly is to _____.

3. To be in an area among other people is to be _____.

4. When something is _____ one group or a place, it happens only in that group or area.

5. The state of being married or unmarried is a person's _____.

6. A sign or object that represents a person, thing, or idea is _____ it.

7. If you dress in a certain way in order to say something about yourself, you _____.

C. *Now use the phrases in your own sentences.*

EXAMPLE: *I took a plane instead of driving because I wanted to* save time.

USE

Work with a partner to answer the questions. Use complete sentences.

1. What are three annoying things that some people do *in public*?
2. How do people in your culture show that they are *in mourning*?
3. What object or fashion is *a symbol of* something else? Explain what it means.
4. What are two things that people wear that are often *fake*?
5. How do people use their clothing to *reveal* their emotions? Describe two ways.
6. Do you like to *make a fashion statement* with your clothing or hair? Explain.
7. Have you ever *imitated* a famous person's hairstyle or clothing? Describe what you did.
8. What modern fashions *demonstrate* the feelings or beliefs of today's teenagers?

COMPREHENSION

UNDERSTANDING MAIN IDEAS

Look at the reading to find the answers to the following questions.

1. What is the main idea of paragraph 1?

    _____

2. Which sentence contains the main idea of paragraph 4?

    _____

3. Which sentence states the main idea of paragraph 7?

    _____

4. What place have wigs had in the history of hair?

    _____

5. What part did the popularity of movies and television play in the history of hair?

    _____

REMEMBERING DETAILS

Reread the passage and fill in the blanks

1. In England and France, wigs were powdered white because _____ .
2. In Africa, brides in the Maasai tribe have their heads shaved as part of their

    _____ .

(continued)

3. A recent popular hairstyle was _____, which an actress on the TV show *Friends* had.

4. During the reign of Queen Elizabeth I, the rich men and women of England dyed their hair _____.

5. Before Assyrian soldiers went to war, they _____.

6. In the 1920s and 1930s, women cut their hair as a symbol of _____.

7. Monks often shave their heads to show _____.

8. In the late 1700s, women had to "open the hair" of their elaborate hairstyles in order to _____.

MAKING INFERENCES

The answers to these questions can be inferred, or guessed, from the reading. Circle the letter of the best answer.

1. The reading implies that in the past _____.
   a. wealth had little to do with how people wore their hair
   b. the wealthy usually had more simple hairstyles than the common people
   c. royalty often started new fashions in hair
   d. people with wealth and status did not consider hairstyles important

2. It can be inferred from the reading that _____.
   a. the only purpose of hair styling has been to make people more beautiful
   b. hair styling has only been popular in modern times
   c. only advanced cultures have been interested in styling their hair
   d. people have always styled their hair for more reasons than beauty

3. From the reading, it can be concluded that _____.
   a. ideas about style and beauty have not changed much over time
   b. we can learn a lot about a culture from the hairstyles of its people
   c. hair styling is not as important today as it was in the past
   d. hairstyles tell us very little about society in general

4. The reading implies that in the 1700s, hairstyles _____.

   a. were not important

   b. were only for women

   c. were ridiculously elaborate

   d. had nothing to do with beauty

5. It can be inferred from the reading that in ancient times, hairstyles _____.

   a. were a symbol of power

   b. were the same in most cultures

   c. were used only for practical reasons

   d. were very simple

DISCUSSION

Discuss the answers to these questions with your classmates.

1. How have hairstyles changed in your country over the last hundred years?

2. Describe the current hairstyles in your country for men, women, children, and older adults. What do these hairstyles say about your culture?

3. Why do young people like to wear new hairstyles?

4. What are some common influences on people's choices of clothes and hairstyles today? What are some of the things that influence you?

CRITICAL THINKING

Work with a partner. Ask each other the following questions. Discuss your answers.

1. Do you spend a lot of time on your clothes and hair? Why or why not? Who spends the most time on personal grooming? Who spends the least time? Is there too much emphasis on style and beauty today? Why or why not?

2. Discuss how each of the following factors influences how a person wears his or her hair: climate, occupation, religion, culture, ethnicity, personality, age, sex, social class.

WRITING

On separate paper, write a paragraph or an essay about one of the following topics.

1. What factors influence young people's choice of hairstyle or clothes?

2. What hairstyles or clothes are or have been extreme to the point of ridicule? Explain.

3. What styles are or have reflected economic or social changes?

GRAMMAR AND PUNCTUATION

COMMAS AFTER INTRODUCTORY WORDS AND PHRASES

We usually use a comma to set off introductory words or phrases at the beginning of a sentence. The comma shows that we pause after we say these words. Remember that a phrase does not have a subject and a verb.

__Throughout history__, hair has always made a fashion statement.
__In almost all societies__, people have cut or styled their hair.
__Finally__, they decorated the hair with jewels, feathers, and ornaments.

Add commas to the following sentences where necessary.

1. As the popularity of movies grew, people copied the hairstyles of movie stars.

2. A few years ago young women copied the hairstyle of Jennifer Aniston, who appeared on the TV show *Friends*.

3. Today's hairstyles express people's personalities.

4. In ancient Egypt women shaved their heads for cleanliness.

5. In some parts of the world hair can reveal marital status, age, or even emotion.

6. At one time all the middle- and upper-class men and women in England wore wigs.

7. Women of high rank in ancient Egypt wore fake beards.

8. By cutting their hair short women showed their liberation.

9. He colored his hair to look younger.

10. In time wigs that were very elaborate went out of fashion.

 Go to page 169 for the Internet Activity.

Go to page 169 for the Internet Activity.

DID YOU KNOW?	• From one strand of hair, scientists can determine what you eat, if you smoke, and what your ethnic origin is. But what they can't tell is your gender. • Studies show that boys' hair grows faster than girls' hair.	

HOW DID CHOPSTICKS ORIGINATE?

before

you read

Answer these questions.

1. In which countries do people use chopsticks?
2. How long have people used chopsticks?
3. Do you ever eat with chopsticks?

HOW DID CHOPSTICKS ORIGINATE?

1   In the beginning, people used just their fingers to eat. Then came the finger-and-knife combination. Around 5,000 years ago, while the rest of the world was still using fingers and a knife, the Chinese began using chopsticks. Today many people eat with a combination of knives, spoons, and forks, but chopsticks are still as important and popular as they were centuries ago.

2   No one knows exactly when the Chinese began to use chopsticks. **According to** one Chinese legend, the use of chopsticks began when two poor farmers were **thrown out** of their village. The farmers went from village to village, but were not welcome anywhere. The two men grew tired and hungry, so they stole a piece of meat from a storeroom in a small village. Then they ran from the village and into a forest, where they quickly made a fire to cook their meat. The smell of the roasting meat was so good that the two men could not wait any longer. Using some sticks from the forest floor, they took the pieces of meat from the fire and put them into their mouths. And so began the custom of chopsticks. Other people did the same, and in a short time people all over China were eating with chopsticks.

3   There are other ideas about why the Chinese started using chopsticks. Some people believe that the philosopher Confucius influenced how the Chinese thought about many things, including how they ate. Confucius, a vegetarian, said it was wrong to have knives at the table because knives were used for killing. Another idea is that there was not enough **fuel** in China. There was only a small amount of fuel available for the cooking of food. But the Chinese **found the solution**! They cut up the food into small pieces before cooking, so it would cook as quickly as possible and only use a very small amount of fuel. The small pieces of food were well suited for chopsticks. It is not certain which came first—chopsticks or the **unique** style of Chinese cooking. But it is certain that chopsticks did have a great influence on the development of Chinese cooking.

4   Chopsticks spread from China to Vietnam and Korea and **eventually** reached Japan by the year 500. Over 3,000 years and between different cultures, several **variations** of chopsticks developed. Chinese chopsticks are nine to ten inches long and round or square at the top end. The Vietnamese did not change the Chinese chopsticks, but the Koreans made their chopsticks a little thinner and then started to make them from metal. Korea is the only country today that uses metal chopsticks. The Japanese made their chopsticks rounded and pointed. They are also shorter—7 inches long for females and 8 inches long for males.

5   Every kind of material is used to make chopsticks. The vast majority of chopsticks are made from bamboo. Bamboo is cheap, **heat resistant**, and has no taste or **odor**. The wealthy have had chopsticks made from gold, jade, ivory, and silver. Some people had strong feelings about some of these materials. In fact,

people once believed silver chopsticks would turn black if they touched any poison. An emperor who was afraid of being poisoned made his servants test each of the dishes with silver chopsticks before he ate. The emperor himself would not use silver chopsticks to eat; he thought the metal in his mouth was unpleasant. Today we know that silver doesn't **react to** poisons, but if bad eggs, onions, or garlic are used, the chemicals might change the color of silver chopsticks.

6   The Japanese made chopsticks from every kind of tree. They even started to put lacquer, a kind of shiny paint, on chopsticks about 400 years ago. The lacquered chopsticks of modern Japan have designs and are beautiful to look at. They are given as special gifts because they are not only beautiful, but **durable**. The layers of lacquer make them last **forever**. The Wajima Nuri area in Japan is famous for making chopsticks with between 75 and 120 separate layers of lacquer. These chopsticks are harder than metal and can cost up to $125 a pair.

7   In 1878, the Japanese were also the first to make **disposable** wooden chopsticks. The disposable chopstick started when a Japanese schoolteacher named Tadao Shimamoto had packed his lunch and brought it to school with him but had **left behind** his pair of chopsticks. Fortunately, his school was in an area of Japan famous for its wood. He explained his problem to one of the local men. The man gave him a piece of wood from which Tadao made a pair of chopsticks. Anyone who has eaten in a Japanese or Chinese restaurant knows what these look like. People liked his chopsticks so much that soon the local area started to produce large numbers of disposable chopsticks called *wari-bashi*. We do not know if Tadao made any money from wari-bashi, but certainly his name is remembered. Each year representatives from disposable chopstick manufacturers go to Tadao's **hometown** and perform a ceremony **in honor of** the father of wari-bashi.

8   About one-half of disposable chopsticks are produced in Japan; the rest come from China, Indonesia, Korea, and the Philippines. Japan uses about 24 billion pairs of disposable chopsticks a year, which is a lot of wood. In fact, it is enough to build over 10,000 homes. Japan now is trying to **eliminate** them for environmental reasons. Today, increasing numbers of Japanese are trying to help the environment. They carry their own personal chopsticks to restaurants instead of using disposable ones. But no matter what kind people use, chopsticks are here to stay.

VOCABULARY

MEANING

Circle the letter of the answer that is closest in meaning to the underlined word.

1. Chopsticks <u>eventually</u> reached Japan by the year 500.
   a. in the course of time
   b. in a short time
   c. at an earlier time
   d. at the right time

2. In 1878, the Japanese were the first to make <u>disposable</u> wooden chopsticks.
   a. made to be used many times
   b. made to be folded and put away
   c. made to be used in a restaurant
   d. made to be used once and thrown away

3. Japan now is trying to <u>eliminate</u> disposable chopsticks for environmental reasons.
   a. increase the number of
   b. get rid of
   c. limit the use of
   d. make copies of

4. It is not certain which came first—chopsticks or the <u>unique</u> style of Chinese cooking.
   a. like many others
   b. very old and traditional
   c. unlike any other
   d. not as good as others

5. Lacquered chopsticks are given as special gifts because they are not only beautiful, but also <u>durable</u>.
   a. heavy
   b. lasting
   c. delicate
   d. elegant

6. There was not enough <u>fuel</u> in China.
   a. equipment that is used during the cooking process
   b. tools that are used to eat meals
   c. material that is burned to produce heat or power
   d. wood that is used to carve bowls and spoons

7. Bamboo has no taste or <u>odor</u>.
   a. smell
   b. shape
   c. color
   d. strength

8. Representatives go to Tadao's <u>hometown</u> and perform a ceremony.
   a. place where he grew up
   b. place where he worked
   c. place where he died
   d. place where he went to school

9. The layers of lacquer make them last <u>forever</u>.

    a. for a short while   **c.** for one time

    b. for a long while   **d.** for all time

10. Several <u>variations</u> of chopsticks developed.

    a. parts   **c.** uses

    b. imitations   **d.** different types

WORDS THAT GO TOGETHER

A. *Find words in the reading that go together with the words below to make phrases.*

1. left _____

2. react _____

3. thrown _____

4. _____ honor _____

5. _____ resistant

6. according _____

7. _____ the solution

B. *Complete the sentences with the phrases from Part A.*

1. When someone is _____ of a place, he is forced to leave because of bad behavior.

2. _____ means "as said by someone" or "as shown by something."

3. To _____ something means to experience a change when coming in contact with it.

4. If you _____, you figured out the answer to a problem.

5. If someone _____ something, they forgot to bring it.

6. To do something _____ someone is to show respect for that person.

7. If something is _____, it will not get hot, even when it gets near a fire or other source of heat.

(continued)

C. *Now use the phrases in your own sentences.*

EXAMPLE: According to *the weather service, it's going to rain tomorrow.*

USE

Work with a partner to answer the questions. Use complete sentences.

1. What kind of food has a strong *odor*?
2. What kind of *fuel* is used to cook in your home?
3. What are two *variations* in how your favorite food is cooked?
4. What are two types of materials that are very *durable*?
5. Where is your *hometown*? Describe it.
6. What do you use that is *disposable*?
7. What experience have you had that you wish would last *forever*?
8. Where are some places that someone might be *thrown out* of for bad behavior?

COMPREHENSION

UNDERSTANDING MAIN IDEAS

Look at the reading to find the answers to the following questions.

1. Which sentence contains the main idea of paragraph 2?

   _____

2. Which sentence states the main idea of paragraph 4?

   _____

3. What is the main idea of paragraph 7?

   _____

4. How did chopsticks solve a problem in China?

   _____

5. Why have disposable chopsticks become a problem in Japan?

   _____

REMEMBERING DETAILS

Reread the passage and circle the letter of the best answer.

1. Japanese chopsticks are _____.
   - **a.** 9 to 10 inches long
   - **b.** thin and made of metal
   - **c.** the same as Chinese chopsticks
   - **d.** rounded and pointed

2. Disposable chopsticks were first made by _____.

   a. a Japanese schoolteacher

   b. two poor Chinese farmers

   c. Confucius

   d. the Koreans

3. Chopsticks are NOT made from _____.

   a. metal

   b. paper

   c. bamboo

   d. jade

4. The Chinese began using chopsticks _____.

   a. in the year 500

   b. about 3,000 years ago

   c. around 5,000 years ago

   d. in 1878

5. The emperor would not use silver chopsticks because he _____.

   a. thought they would poison his food

   b. thought they would turn his tongue black

   c. only wanted chopsticks made from gold

   d. didn't like the metallic taste

6. The Japanese give gifts of beautiful chopsticks made with many layers of _____.

   a. bamboo

   b. lacquer

   c. metal

   d. ivory

7. In the Chinese style of cooking, food is _____ before it is cooked.

   a. cut into small pieces

   b. tested for poison

   c. placed on an open fire

   d. mixed with onions and garlic

8. Confucius was a Chinese _____.

   a. schoolteacher

   b. cook

   c. emperor

   d. philosopher

MAKING INFERENCES

Some of the following statements are facts from the reading. Other statements can be inferred, or guessed. Write F *for each factual statement. Write* I *for each inference.*

_____ 1. When two poor farmers used sticks to pick up hot meat, they had no idea that they were starting a new method of eating in China.

(continued)

_____ 2. Confucius was a vegetarian, and he said it was wrong to have knives at the table because knives were used for killing.

_____ 3. Chopsticks are not suitable for eating all types of food.

_____ 4. Chopsticks are made from many different types of materials.

_____ 5. People believed that silver chopsticks would turn black if they touched poison, but today we know that isn't true.

_____ 6. The most famous area in Japan for making lacquered chopsticks is Wajima Nuri.

_____ 7. Tadao Shimamoto wasn't trying to create a new product for sale when he made his first pair of disposable chopsticks.

_____ 8. Disposable chopsticks are very useful to people but are not so good for the world in which we live.

_____ 9. Chopsticks don't work very well for cutting or picking up large pieces of food.

_____ 10. In Japan, men and women use different lengths of chopsticks.

DISCUSSION

Discuss the answers to these questions with your classmates.

1. Today, we use a lot of disposable things that are bad for the environment. Should we stop using some disposable items? Which ones?

2. What are some dos and don'ts for eating at the table in your country?

3. What are the advantages and/or disadvantages of these three ways of eating: with fingers; with fork, knife, and spoon; with chopsticks? Which do you prefer? Why?

4. What steps can we take to protect our environment?

CRITICAL THINKING

Work with a partner. Ask each other the following questions. Discuss your answers.

1. How does the way in which food is served, and what it is served on or in, affect how the food tastes and how much you enjoy it? What are your favorite foods? What are some things that make you enjoy a meal more?

2. Some people think that Confucius influenced how the Chinese ate. In the past in your country, what were some influences on the types of food people ate and how they were prepared and served? How does the modern world influence what, how, and where we eat? In your own life, what are the greatest influences on your eating habits?

WRITING

On separate paper, write a paragraph or an essay about one of the following topics.

1. What are the advantages and/or disadvantages of using disposable products?
2. Describe how you usually serve and eat food in your country.
3. What are the advantages and/or disadvantages of eating fast foods?

GRAMMAR AND PUNCTUATION

HYPHENS

We use a hyphen (-) to form compound words (words made by combining two or more words) and to join prefixes and suffixes to root words.

(Note: The use of the hyphen in compound words changes over time. As a compound word becomes more common, we stop hyphenating it. It is always a good idea to check in a dictionary if you are not sure.)

We usually use a hyphen:

- for fractions and compound numbers from twenty-one to ninety-nine
  one-half *of the chopsticks*   **seventy-five** *layers of lacquer*

- with the prefixes *all-*, *ex-*, and *self-*
  all-*powerful*   **ex-***president*   **self-***service*

- with all prefixes before a proper noun or a proper adjective
  post-*World War II*   **pro-***Japanese*

- to connect certain compound nouns
  stir-fry   **good-bye**

- to connect compound adjectives that come before a noun
  a **heat-resistant** *wood*   *an* **old-fashioned** *restaurant*

A. *Correct the errors in hyphen use. Add hyphens where necessary.*

1. one third of grown ups

   _____

2. one-hundred and twenty five million

   _____

3. a left handed-person

   _____

(continued)

4. bite sized pieces

_____

5. hand polished chopsticks

_____

6. anti disposable chopstick campaign

_____

B. *Find and correct the errors in hyphen use. Then compare answers with a partner.*

Koreans love short grain sticky rice. There is always some rice that sticks to the bottom of the cooking pot. When Koreans serve dinner, they add enough water to cover the stuck on rice (about three fourths of a cup). They leave this to cook through the dinner. After dinner, the rice water tea is drunk in the same way as the Western after dinner coffee.

 Go to page 169 for the Internet Activity.

<table>
<tr><td>DID
YOU
KNOW?</td><td>• **Don't cross your chopsticks. This is a symbol of death.**
• **Don't stick chopsticks into your food—especially rice. This is only done at funerals.**
• **Thirty percent of the world's population uses chopsticks.**</td><td></td></tr>
</table>

WHERE DID CERTAIN WEDDING CUSTOMS COME FROM?

you read

before

Answer these questions.

1. Do you like to attend weddings? Why or why not?
2. What are some wedding customs in your country?
3. Do you prefer a traditional or modern wedding? Why?

Where Did Certain Wedding Customs Come From?

1   Everywhere around the world, weddings are celebrated with some kind of ceremony. These ceremonies differ between cultures, but many of the customs **associated with** wedding ceremonies—such as the wedding ring, the wedding dress, the wedding cake, and throwing confetti—come from common beliefs and similar ancient traditions.

2   The idea of the wedding ring started with the ancient Hindus. It was not considered to be a symbol of love in the beginning. It was, in fact, a sign that a **down payment** had been given for the woman and that she was no longer **available**. In some tribes in Africa, women are still bought. In 1964, a chief of the Maasai tribe offered 150 cows, 20 goats, and $750 cash to buy American actress Carroll Baker. This was a lot, **considering** the best Maasai fighter then paid $200 and 12 cows for a wife!

3   The ancient Greeks and Romans took the idea of wedding rings from the Hindus, and they also kept the ring as a sign that a young lady was "sold." Christian societies **adopted** the ring around the year 1000 as a sign of **fidelity**. The ring, a circle with no beginning and no end, also was a symbol of **eternity**. The Scandinavians did not adopt the custom of wedding rings until the late 1600s. Before then, they preferred to break a gold or silver coin and have each partner keep one half.

4   There are also various beliefs about which hand and finger to put the ring on. The ancient Greeks and Romans wore the ring on the fourth finger of the left hand because they believed that a **vein** ran directly to the heart from that finger. However, wedding rings are not worn on the left hand in every country. In Chile and Germany, couples exchange rings when they get engaged, wear their rings on their left hand until they are married, and then **switch** them to their right hands. In Russia, there is no special finger for a wedding ring. However, people there usually wear a ring on the right hand to **indicate** they have a partner. In some countries, like Brazil, couples wear rings on the left hand and have their names inscribed inside the ring: the bride has the groom's name on her ring and **vice versa**. In Sweden, women wear three rings: one for engagement, one for marriage, and one for motherhood.

5   Today many brides marry in a white dress, which symbolizes purity. This tradition started in the 1500s. Before that time, brides wore their best dress, and the color **did not matter**. Today, in the United States and Britain, brides wear white dresses and follow the tradition of wearing "something old, something new, something borrowed, something blue." Each "something" has a special meaning.

"Something old" is a symbol of past happiness and symbolizes the transfer of these feelings to the bride's marriage. "Something new" symbolizes the hoped for success of the marriage, and it often takes the form of a new dress. "Something borrowed" represents the hope that the loyalty of friends will continue through the marriage, and "something blue" stands for fidelity, since blue is the color that symbolizes this value. In Japan, white was always the color for a bride even before it became popular in Western cultures. A Japanese bride may sometimes change her dress two or three times on her wedding day. She may start with a traditional kimono and end with a Western-style white dress. In Finland, brides wear white dresses and golden crowns. After the wedding ceremony, guests cover the bride's eyes, and the unmarried women dance around her as she puts the crown on one of their heads. Whomever she crowns, it is believed, will be the next bride.

6   White is not the color worn by brides everywhere. In China and Pakistan, brides wear red, which symbolizes happiness. In Samoa, brides wear a dress made of material from the bark of a tree, along with fresh flowers and a crown of mother of pearl. In the past, it was **common practice** in many cultures for the bride and the bridesmaids to wear the same color as a way of confusing evil spirits that might hurt the bride. Today, this tradition is still present in the Philippines.

7   The idea of the wedding cake is common throughout the world. Originally, the wedding cake was not eaten by the bride. It was thrown at her! People thought that throwing cake at a bride would bring her **fertility**. It originally started with throwing wheat, which later took the form of little cakes. Later, the cakes were **piled** on top of each other, and a higher pile meant more prosperity for the couple. Finally, a French chef thought of the multilayered cake that is common in Western cultures today. Many countries have their own traditional cakes: the Irish have a fruitcake, in Ukraine it is a wedding bread, in Denmark it is an almond cake with beautifully decorated sugar work, and in France they have caramel-coated cream puffs.

8   Throwing things at the couple to wish them fertility or prosperity is also common throughout different cultures. People in the United States traditionally threw rice at couples as they left the place where they got married. When people learned that the rice was making birds sick, they began throwing birdseed. Unfortunately, the seeds injured some brides and grooms. Therefore, Americans today often blow bubbles or throw confetti, which is a mix of small pieces of colored paper, often in the form of hearts, horseshoes, and slippers. (The word *confetti* comes from an Italian word meaning "sweetmeats," which are mixed nuts, dried fruit, and honeyed almonds.)

9   Of course, there are variations to this tradition: Italians throw sugared almonds to symbolize the sweet (sugar) and bitter parts of life; in the Czech Republic, people throw peas; in Romania, it's sweets and nuts. Throwing shoes once was preferred over throwing wheat, rice, or birdseed, because in the old days people believed shoes were a symbol of fertility. The Inuit of North America still have this tradition. It is also common today in the United States and Britain to tie shoes to the back of the newlyweds' car.

(continued)

10   Even in our modern traditions, we still use ancient symbols to show our wishes for marriage unions to be happy and fruitful. Most of these wedding customs from around the world have things **in common** and come from shared human values. Though many customs are based on ancient traditions and superstitions that we may not **be aware of** today, they have the same purpose: They all celebrate marriage and wish the new couple well.

VOCABULARY

MEANING

Circle the letter of the answer that is closest in meaning to the underlined word.

1. People thought that throwing cake at a bride would bring her <u>fertility</u>.
   a. the talent to make money
   b. the good health to live a long life
   c. the ability to have babies
   d. the faithfulness to have a good marriage

2. Christian societies <u>adopted</u> the ring around the year 1000.
   a. began to use or have
   b. put aside
   c. refused to accept
   d. changed according to their wishes

3. Ancient Greeks and Romans wore the ring on the fourth finger of the left hand because they believed that a <u>vein</u> ran directly to the heart from that finger.
   a. a nerve that sends signals
   b. a tube that carries blood
   c. a muscle that makes movement
   d. an organ that beats quickly

4. Later, the cakes were <u>piled</u> on top of each other.
   a. put side by side
   b. covered by something
   c. placed one on the other
   d. separated into groups

5. This was a lot, <u>considering</u> the best Maasai fighter paid $200 and 12 cows for a wife.
   a. comparing
   b. wondering about
   c. forgetting about
   d. keeping in mind

6. People in Russia usually wear a ring on the right hand to <u>indicate</u> they have a partner.
   a. design
   b. describe
   c. show
   d. remind

7. It was a sign that the woman was no longer <u>available</u>.
   a. free to begin a romance
   b. attractive to other men
   c. young enough for marriage
   d. valuable to own

8. Christian societies adopted the ring as a sign of <u>fidelity</u>.
   a. faithfulness
   b. love
   c. friendship
   d. good fortune

9. The ring was also was a symbol of <u>eternity</u>.
   a. a number of years
   b. the present time
   c. time without end
   d. a moment

10. After they are married, they <u>switch</u> their rings to their right hands.
    a. take off
    b. change
    c. turn over
    d. hold

WORDS THAT GO TOGETHER

A. *Find words in the reading that go together with the words below to make phrases.*

1. _____ practice
2. _____ payment
3. _____ versa
4. associated _____
5. _____ aware _____
6. _____ common
7. _____ matter

B. *Complete the sentences with the phrases from Part A.*

1. When people or things share something, such as a quality or interest, they are thought to have it _____.

2. _____ means "in the opposite way."

3. When something _____, it was not important.

4. Something that is done often by many people is _____.

5. Things that are related, or connected, are _____ each other.

6. When you pay part of the price for something in order to hold it as your future possession, you are giving a _____ for that property.

7. To _____ something is to have understanding of it.

C. *Now use the phrases in your own sentences.*

EXAMPLE: *It is* common practice *in my company to reward good workers.*

USE

Work with a partner to answer the questions. Use complete sentences.

1. What are two kinds of purchases that often require a *down payment*?
2. What does *fidelity* between two people mean?
3. What are two items that are made of things *piled* on each other?
4. What is a holiday custom that is *common practice* in your culture?
5. What famous person would you like to *switch* lives with?
6. How can someone with a partner or spouse show that he or she is no longer *available*?
7. What kinds of celebrations do most societies have *in common*?
8. What is a custom that your culture has *adopted* from another culture?

COMPREHENSION

UNDERSTANDING MAIN IDEAS

Some of the following statements are main ideas and some are supporting statements. Some of them are stated directly in the reading. Find the statements. Write M for each main idea. Write S for each supporting statement.

_____ 1. In Sweden, women wear three rings: one for engagement, one for marriage, and one for motherhood.

_____ 2. Today many brides marry in a white dress, which symbolizes purity.

_____ 3. The idea of the wedding cake is common throughout the world.

_____ 4. "Something borrowed" represents the hope that the loyalty of friends will continue through the marriage.

_____ 5. There are also various beliefs about which hand and finger to put the ring on.

REMEMBERING DETAILS

Reread the passage and circle the letter of the best answer.

1. The multilayered cake common in Western cultures today was first created by _____.
   a. an American bride
   b. a man in Ukraine
   c. a French chef
   d. a baker in Denmark

2. In the old days, people believed shoes were a symbol of _____.
   a. prosperity
   b. faithfulness
   c. happiness
   d. fertility

3. The idea of the wedding ring started with the ancient _____.
   a. Greeks
   b. Romans
   c. African tribes
   d. Hindus

4. The Japanese bride may start her wedding day by wearing a _____.
   a. traditional kimono
   b. Western-style white dress
   c. white dress and golden crown
   d. red dress

5. In many cultures, the bride and bridesmaids wore the same colors in order to _____.
   a. play tricks on the groom
   b. confuse evil spirits
   c. bring the bride fertility
   d. show the faithfulness of friends

6. In Brazil, engaged couples wear rings _____.
   a. inscribed with each other's names
   b. on their right hands
   c. on no special finger
   d. in groups of three

7. In the Czech Republic, people throw _____ at the new couple.
   a. sugared almonds
   b. sweets and nuts
   c. peas
   d. rice

8. In Ukraine, the traditional wedding cake is _____.
   a. an almond cake
   b. caramel-coated cream puffs
   c. a multilayered cake
   d. a bread

MAKING INFERENCES

Some of the following statements can be inferred, or guessed, from the reading and others cannot. Circle the number of each statement that can be inferred.

1. Although the wearing of the wedding ring differs among cultures, the meaning of the ring is similar.
2. The use of the wedding ring is a fairly modern custom.
3. Most cultures have always considered it wrong to think of a bride as property.
4. Most wedding ceremonies combine traditional and modern customs.

(continued)

5. The color of a bride's dress is not important in most cultures.

6. Many wedding customs are related to the desire for a new couple to have children.

7. The wedding cake can take many forms.

8. The idea of throwing things at a couple is not very popular today.

DISCUSSION

Discuss the answers to these questions with your classmates.

1. Some people marry without a wedding celebration. Which way do you prefer? Why?

2. Besides a ring, what are some other symbols of love in today's world?

3. Why are wedding customs important to a couple? What purpose do they serve?

4. If you were getting married, what kind of wedding would you like to have?

CRITICAL THINKING

Work with a partner. Ask each other the following questions. Discuss your answers.

1. What kind of wedding vows do the people in your culture exchange? What is the purpose of wedding vows? Why do some couples today write their own vows? Which do you prefer, traditional or self-written vows? Why?

2. What is the purpose of marriage? With so many divorces today, is marriage outdated? Why or why not? Many Western couples live decades together and have children without getting married. What is your opinion of this? Which do you prefer, to be single or married? What are the advantages and disadvantages of each?

WRITING

On separate paper, write a paragraph or an essay about one of the following topics:

1. Describe three or four steps before a wedding takes place in your country.

2. Describe in three or four steps the wedding ceremony in your country.

3. Describe the traditional wedding dress, ring, and cake in your country.

GRAMMAR AND PUNCTUATION

COMMAS TO SEPARATE INTERRUPTERS

Interrupters are expressions that create a pause in the flow of the sentence. We separate interrupters from the rest of the sentence by putting commas before and/or after them. These are some common interrupters:

after all	by the way	I believe	indeed
as we all know	for example	I think	naturally
as far as we know	however	in fact	of course

In fact, the wedding ring was a sign that a down payment had been given for the bride.

*Whoever she crowns, **it is believed**, will be the next bride.*

*There are variations to this tradition, **of course**.*

Add commas to the following sentences where necessary.

1. Most brides in Western cultures, as we all know wear white.
2. White however is not the color worn by brides everywhere.
3. As far as we know the idea of a wedding ring started with the ancient Hindus.
4. In Chile for example, couples wear wedding rings on their right hands.
5. Swedish women wear three rings by the way.
6. The girl who catches the bridal bouquet it is believed will be the next bride.
7. Naturally when people threw rice at the couple some brides and grooms got injured.
8. The Inuit of North America still use shoes as a fertility symbol for example.
9. Indeed many wedding customs are from old traditions and superstitions.
10. The purpose of all these customs after all is to wish the new couple well.

Go to page 170 for the Internet Activity.

Go to page 170 for the Internet Activity.

DID YOU KNOW?

- The origin of the wedding shower is based on a legend of a Dutch girl who fell in love with a poor miller. Her family could not afford a dowry so her friends "showered" them with gifts so they could be married without a dowry.
- Many cultures believe that loud noises can scare evil spirits away. That is why today people honk their horns when they see the bride or when the couple leaves the wedding ceremony.
- People believed in evil spirits in ancient times. A man carried his bride to protect her from the evil spirits on the ground, which may be the origin of the custom of carrying the bride over the threshold.

SELF-TEST 1

Units 1–8

A. COMPREHENSION

Circle the letter of the correct answer.

1. A Medieval castle provided people with _____.
   a. a warm, comfortable place to live
   b. a protected and easy way of life
   c. a safe but cold and unclean place to live
   d. a dangerous and difficult place to live

2. Life in Inca society was _____.
   a. organized and controlled
   b. cruel and inhuman
   c. full of chaos and confusion
   d. happy and carefree

3. The Diwali festival celebrates _____.
   a. the harvest and a time when food is plentiful
   b. new beginnings and the triumph of good over evil
   c. the family and the importance of humility and sacrifice
   d. the gods with religious services and days of quiet prayer and meditation

4. *The 1,001 Arabian Nights* is _____.
   a. the true story of a woman named Scheherazade
   b. a long poem depicting life in early Arabia
   c. a history of King Shahryar and his court
   d. a collection of folk tales from many countries

5. Angkor Wat is remarkable because of _____.
   a. its size and the way it was built
   b. its location in the jungle
   c. why it was built and what it was used for
   d. the history of the people who built it

6. Hair styles have _____.
   a. not changed much over time
   b. only been important to people in modern times
   c. always revealed things about people and culture
   d. historically been important only for beauty and decoration

7. Chopsticks _____.
   a. have always been made from the same materials
   b. are exactly alike everywhere in the world
   c. are used for many different purposes
   d. have different designs and materials

8. Wedding customs are _____.
   a. no longer important in modern Western countries
   b. similar around the world but have different meanings and purposes
   c. different around the world but have similar purposes
   d. something that started in modern times

B. VOCABULARY

Complete the sentences. Circle the letter of the correct answer.

1. The lord of the castle _____ his daily business in the great hall.
   a. put away   b. carried out   c. soaked up   d. passed down

2. The Incas had a(n) _____ system of roads.
   a. inferior   b. sophisticated   c. industrialized   d. piled

3. In India, Diwali is a time when light _____ over darkness.
   a. implores   b. honors   c. triumphs   d. rejoices

4. *The 1,001 Arabian Nights* _____ what life was like in those times.
   a. depicts   b. imitates   c. encounters   d. intimidates

5. Other people came to steal _____ from the temple.
   a. artifacts   b. inscriptions   c. diaries   d. stones

(continued)

6. At one time, hairstyles became extravagant to the point of _____.

    a. status   **b.** privileges   **c.** ridicule   **d.** prosperity

7. Today, Japan is trying to _____ the use of disposable chopsticks for environmental reasons.

    a. neglect   **b.** demonstrate   **c.** eliminate   **d.** switch

8. Christians used the wedding ring as a sign of _____.

    a. fidelity   **b.** attitude   **c.** significance   **d.** reluctance

C. GRAMMAR AND PUNCTUATION

Circle the letter of the sentence or sentences with the correct grammar and punctuation.

1. **a.** The lord of the castle, together with his family, were the only ones to have a bedroom.

    b. The lord of the castle, together with his family, was the only one to have a bedroom.

    c. The lord of the castle and his family was the only one to have a bedroom.

    d. The lord of the castle and his family were the only one to have a bedroom.

2. **a.** The Incas had huge storehouses all over the country. Therefore no one starved.

    b. The Incas had huge storehouses all over the country. No one, therefore starved.

    c. The Incas had huge storehouses all over the country. Therefore, no one starved.

    d. The Incas had huge storehouses all over the country. No one starved therefore.

3. **a.** Diwali she said is a time to be happy and enjoy family and friends.

    b. "Diwali," she said, "is a time to be happy and enjoy family and friends."

    c. Diwali she said "is a time to be happy and enjoy family and friends."

    d. "Diwali she said is a time to be happy and enjoy family and friends."

4. **a.** While the dazzled king listened, Scheherazade stopped at the most exciting part of the story.

    b. While the dazzling king listened, Scheherazade stopped at the most exciting part of the story.

    c. While the dazzled king listened, Scheherazade stopped at the most excited part of the story.

    d. While the dazzling king listened, Scheherazade stopping at the most excited part of the story.

5. **a.** The temple was built as a Hindu temple, however, it later became a Buddhist temple.

   b. The temple was built as a Hindu temple; however, it later became a Buddhist temple.

   c. The temple was built as a Hindu temple; It later became a Buddhist temple.

   d. The temple was built as a Hindu temple; But it later became a Buddhist temple.

6. **a.** In ancient Egypt, men and women shaved their heads for cleanliness.

   b. In ancient Egypt men and women shaved their heads for cleanliness.

   c. In ancient Egypt men and women, shaved their heads for cleanliness.

   d. In ancient Egypt men and women shaved their heads, for cleanliness.

7. a. In many Asian countries, food is cut into bite-size pieces and stir-fried.

   b. In many Asian countries, food is cut into bitesize pieces and stir-fried.

   c. In many Asian countries, food is cut into bite size pieces and stirfried.

   d. In many Asian countries, food is cut into bite-size pieces and stir fried.

8. **a.** Most wedding customs in fact are based on ancient traditions and superstitions.

   b. Most wedding customs, in fact are based on ancient traditions and superstitions.

   c. Most wedding customs, in fact, are based on ancient traditions and superstitions.

   d. In fact most wedding customs are based on ancient traditions and superstitions.

UNIT 9

WHAT IS THE CURSE OF KING TUT?

you read

before

Answer these questions.

1. Where are the tombs of the Egyptian pharaohs?
2. What did the Egyptians put inside the tombs of the pharaohs?
3. What do you know about the legend of the "mummy's curse"?

WHAT IS THE CURSE OF KING TUT?

1   It was 1910 when two Englishmen thought of finding a special tomb in Egypt. This was the tomb of Tutankhamen, called "Tut" for short. The two men were Howard Carter, an archeologist, and Lord Carnarvon, a wealthy man. Carter had the **know-how**, and Lord Carnarvon had the money.

2   Tutankhamen was a pharaoh, or ruler, of ancient Egypt. In about 1300 B.C.E., when he was only a boy of about eight, he became ruler. After ruling for nine years, he died. Like all pharaohs, his body was made into a mummy after he died. A mummy is a dead body that goes through a process to **preserve** it. This process was invented in ancient Egypt. The mummy was then buried in a tomb with the pharaoh's treasures. Over the years, the location of his tomb was forgotten, but Carter and Carnarvon were **convinced** that the tomb was in the Valley of the Kings and wanted to find it. The Valley of the Kings was in the south of Egypt. It was here that pharaohs from the New Kingdom, which began about 1550 B.C.E. and included Tutankhamen, made their tombs and hoped that robbers would not find them.

3   In 1922, Carnarvon wanted to **give up** the search for the tomb. They had already searched for almost five years, and a lot of money had been spent, but nothing was found. Carnarvon called Carter to England and told him he would not pay for any more work. Carter had been expecting this, but persuaded him to fund him for one more year. While he was in England, Carter bought a yellow pet canary. When he went back to Egypt, he took the yellow canary with him. The Egyptians said the bird would **bring luck**.

4   Maybe it did because on November 4, 1922, one of Carter's men discovered hidden steps near where they were digging in the Valley of the Kings. He ran to get Carter, who immediately came to **investigate**. Carter recognized the steps as a stairway to a tomb. Carter was so excited that he ran to his tent to send a telegram to Lord Carnarvon. He told him to come to Egypt right away. Just then he saw a snake—a cobra—eating his canary! He did not think much of this at the time, but people thought this was the beginning of the "Curse of Tutankhamen." Carter cleared the stairway and found that it led to a **sealed** door at the bottom of the steps. The name *Tutankhamen* was found for the first time at the bottom of the doorway.

5   Lord Carnarvon arrived with his daughter at the site a few weeks later. On November 26, he watched as Carter made a hole in the door. Carter **looked through**, holding a candle. Carnarvon asked, "Can you see anything?" "Yes," said Carter, "Wonderful things!" Later, it was found that the tomb was filled with more than 5,000 objects: clothes, jewelry, furniture, and many things that the Egyptians believed a pharaoh might need in his afterlife. There was more. There was a gold coffin and inside it was another coffin smaller than the one before, and finally the mummy of the boy-king Tutankhamen. News of this discovery went all over the

(continued)

world. Carter and Carnarvon **sold the rights to** the story of their discovery to the *London Times* for a large amount of money. The other newspapers and journalists became very angry. Carnarvon and Carter wanted to make up some of the money it had cost them for years of digging, so they **took every opportunity** they could through the sale of photographs or accounts to make money on their discovery.

6   Strange events started to happen. Lord Carnarvon was bitten by a mosquito. He later developed an infection and died five months after the discovery of the tomb. There was a story that said that all the lights of Cairo went out at the **precise** moment Carnarvon died, while in England his dog howled and died at the same time. Even more strange was that when Tutankhamen was unwrapped in 1925, a **wound** was found on his left cheek in the exact position of the mosquito bite on Lord Carnarvon. Journalists started to write that it was the "Curse of the Pharaohs." The curse of the pharaohs was nothing new. Other writers had written books called *The Mummy* or *The Mummy's Curse*, but these were all fictional. There were journalists and other people who wanted to **get** people's **attention** and make money; they started to **speculate** that people were dying because of an ancient curse. Other deaths were connected to the curse: Lord Carnarvon's younger brother died suddenly in 1923. An Egyptologist, A. C. Mace, who worked with Carter, died before his work on the tomb was finished. A French Egyptologist, Georges Bénédite, fell while looking through the tomb and died later from his injuries. An X-ray expert who was on his way to examine the mummy died before he reached Egypt. Carter's secretary suddenly died and the secretary's father, Lord Westbury, killed himself by jumping from a building. He had believed in the curse and wrote, "I cannot stand any more horrors and I am going to make my exit." Any death connected with Egypt was thought to be caused by the curse, even those before the discovery of Tut's tomb. By 1935, there were twenty-one "**victims**" of the curse. Was there really a curse or was it the press turning this into **sensationalism**?

7   Herbert Winlock, the director of the Metropolitan Museum of Art in New York and an Egyptologist, had his own opinion about the belief in the curse. According to him, of the twenty-two people present when the tomb was opened in 1922, only six had died by 1934. All the people who were present at the unwrapping of the mummy, which was the most dangerous time of all, were still alive. Perhaps the curse only affected the people who believed in it. Howard Carter, who actually opened the tomb and put the mummy **on display**, never believed in the curse. He lived for another seventeen years and died naturally. Lord Carnarvon's daughter, who was one of the first people to enter the tomb, lived for another fifty-eight years!

What do you think?

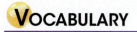

MEANING

Circle the letter of the answer that is closest in meaning to the underlined word.

1. A mummy is a dead body that goes through a process to <u>preserve</u> it.
   a. make something better than it was
   b. take something apart
   c. turn one thing into something else
   d. keep something in good condition

2. Carter and Carnarvon were <u>convinced</u> that the tomb was in the Valley of the Kings.
   a. doubted
   b. wondered
   c. were confused about
   d. believed

3. Carter had the <u>know-how</u>, and Lord Carnarvon had the money.
   a. information
   b. imagination
   c. ability or skill
   d. facts

4. He ran to get Carter, who immediately came to <u>investigate</u>.
   a. look into
   b. talk about
   c. get excited about
   d. cover up

5. Carter found that it led to a <u>sealed</u> door.
   a. closed in a way that could not be easily opened
   b. decorated in a beautiful way
   c. made too small to fit through
   d. written on with an official statement

(continued)

6. All the lights of Cairo went out at the <u>precise</u> moment Carnarvon died.

    a. near

    b. exact

    c. not quite

    d. a bit more

7. A <u>wound</u> was found on the left cheek.

    a. a mark placed on the skin

    b. a damaged place on the body

    c. a jewel put on the body

    d. a light spot on the skin

8. Journalists started to <u>speculate</u> that people were dying because of an ancient curse.

    a. discover

    b. learn

    c. guess

    d. doubt

9. By 1935, there were twenty-one "<u>victims</u>" of the curse.

    a. people who cause harm to others

    b. people who suffer pain or harm

    c. people who make up stories

    d. people who refuse to believe

10. Was it the press turning this into <u>sensationalism</u>?

    a. causing excitement or shock

    b. making things better

    c. calming things down

    d. telling the truth

WORDS THAT GO TOGETHER

A. *Find words in the reading that go together with the words below to make phrases.*

1. sold _____ to

2. give _____

3. _____ . . . attention

4. _____ display

5. _____ through

6. bring-_____

7. _____ every _____

B. _Complete the sentences with the phrases from Part A._

1. When you put something _____, you place it where everyone can see it.

2. When you _____ people's _____, you get them to look at or think about something.

3. If someone _____ something, they got money for allowing someone else to use it.

4. If people used every favorable moment or chance to do or get something, it means that they _____.

5. If you _____ something, you stop having or doing it.

6. If something will _____, it will make good things happen.

7. When you _____ something, you used an opening in it to see something.

C. _Now use the phrases in your own sentences._

EXAMPLE: _I wanted to_ give up _my piano lessons, but my teacher changed my mind._

USE

Work with a partner to answer the questions. Use complete sentences.

1. What are some ways in which you have received a _wound_?

2. What is a recent natural disaster that created many _victims_?

3. What do people _speculate_ are some of the causes of global warming?

4. What is a recent news story that journalists have made into _sensationalism_?

5. If you could _preserve_ something for all time, what would it be?

6. When the police _investigate_ a crime scene, what are some things they look for?

7. How do you usually open a _sealed_ envelope?

8. What special _know-how_ you would like to have?

COMPREHENSION

UNDERSTANDING MAIN IDEAS

Some of the following statements are main ideas and some are supporting statements. Some of them are stated directly in the reading. Find the statements. Write M for each main idea. Write S for each supporting statement.

_____ 1. Tut was a pharaoh whose body was made into a mummy after he died.

_____ 2. At one point, Lord Carnarvon wanted to give up the search for the tomb.

_____ 3. There was a smaller coffin inside a large gold coffin.

_____ 4. Strange things started happening once the tomb was opened.

_____ 5. Howard Carter, who had opened the tomb, never believed in the curse.

REMEMBERING DETAILS

Reread the passage and answer the questions. Write complete sentences.

1. Where did Carter find King Tut's tomb?

_____

2. Why did Carter buy a yellow canary?

_____

3. What happened to Carter's canary?

_____

4. Besides the coffin, what did Carter find in Tut's tomb?

_____

5. Why did Carter and Carnarvon sell the rights to their story?

_____

6. What did someone say happened in England when Carnarvon died?

_____

7. How did French Egyptologist Georges Bénédite die?

_____

8. How many people present when the tomb was opened had actually died by 1934?

_____

MAKING INFERENCES

The answers to these questions can be inferred, or guessed, from the reading. Circle the letter of the best answer.

1. The reading implies that the Egyptians _____.
   a. wanted to forget that the pharaohs ever existed
   b. didn't believe in life after death
   c. wanted to honor and protect their dead pharaohs
   d. took a pharaoh's treasure after he died

2. It can be inferred from the reading that Carter _____.
   a. knew exactly where the tomb was located
   b. didn't want Carnarvon to find the tomb first
   c. believed in his ability to find the tomb
   d. really wanted to stop looking for the tomb

3. From the reading, it can be concluded that publishing the sensational stories of the curse _____.
   a. made people laugh
   b. caused harm to others
   c. was mostly good for readers
   d. was done for a good purpose

4. The reading implies that the curse was _____.
   a. probably true
   b. something made up by Lord Carnarvon
   c. believed by a New York Egyptologist
   d. not based on true facts

DISCUSSION

Discuss the answers to these questions with your classmates.

1. Do you believe in the "mummy's curse"? What are some other curses that are believed to exist? Why and how do you think these legends get started? Why do many people believe them?

(continued)

2. If you could build an elaborate tomb for yourself and put things in it for your use in the afterlife, what would your tomb look like and what would it contain?

3. Many people are fascinated by Egypt and the study of ancient history in general. Why do you think they feel this way? Why do we study ancient history today? What do we hope to learn?

4. What are some movies that have been made about the exciting exploits of archeologists? Do you think that being an archeologist is romantic and exciting? Why or why not? Would you like to be an archeologist? Explain.

CRITICAL THINKING

Work with a partner. Ask each other the following questions. Discuss your answers.

1. What are some other ancient historical places around the world? Is it right to remove artifacts and even human remains from these places and put them in museums? Why or why not? What are the positive aspects of putting artifacts in museums? What are the negatives? Do countries such as Egypt, Italy, and Greece have a right to demand that countries return objects that were stolen or simply taken by archeologists decades ago or even a hundred years ago? Why or why not?

2. Many people today are concerned about sensationalism in the media. Why are they concerned? Is this something that you are concerned with as well? Why or why not? Do you think there's more sensationalism today than in the past? Do reporters exaggerate stories or report more on stories that grab attention rather than reporting on more important issues? Why or why not? What are the negative aspects of sensationalism? Are there any positive aspects? If so, what are they?

WRITING

On separate paper, write a paragraph or an essay about one of the following topics.

1. Write about the pros and cons of believing in curses.
2. Write about the advantages or disadvantages of sensationalism in newspapers.
3. Write about not giving up.

GRAMMAR AND PUNCTUATION

ARTICLES: *A, AN, THE*

Articles give information about a noun. We use *a/an* when the noun is not known to the reader or listener. We use *the* after we know what noun we are talking about. Therefore, we use *a/an* for the first reference and *the* for the next and other references. (Note: We use *an* before a vowel sound.)

*Two Englishmen wanted to find **a tomb**.*
*This was **the tomb** of Tutankhamen.*

We use *the* or no article for plural nouns. We don't use an article when we refer to a group in general.

***Mummies** were an Egyptian invention.*
*They found **the mummies** in the tomb.*

Fill in the blanks with a, an, the, *or* X *for no article.*

1. _____ mummy is _____ dead body that goes through _____ process to preserve it.

2. Howard Carter was _____ archeologist and knew all about _____ tombs.

3. Carter bought _____ canary in England and took _____ canary with him to Egypt.

4. One of the men discovered _____ steps which Carter recognized as _____ stairway.

5. Carter made _____ hole in the door; then he looked through _____ hole.

6. _____ journalists started to write about _____ "Curse of The Pharaohs."

7. Was there _____ curse or was it _____ press trying to make news?

8. Lord Carnarvon had _____ infection and died five months after _____ discovery of _____ tomb.

9. King Tut's tomb was filled with _____ furniture, _____ jewelry, and _____ clothes.

10. Howard Carter, who had opened _____ tomb, never believed in _____ curse.

Go to page 170 for the Internet Activity.

DID YOU KNOW?	• About 3,500 articles were found in the tomb of King Tut. • King Tut married his half sister, which was the custom at the time. • At the time of King Tut, the higher the status of the man, the more wigs he owned. • The inside soles of shoes belonging to the Pharaoh were decorated with images of traditional Egyptian enemies, so he would step on them as he walked.

WHY DO PEOPLE WANT TO CLIMB MOUNT EVEREST?

before you read

Answer these questions.

1. Where is Mount Everest?
2. Who were the first men to successfully climb Mount Everest?
3. Why do people do dangerous things such as climbing mountains?

WHY DO PEOPLE WANT TO CLIMB MOUNT EVEREST?

1 When asked why he wanted to climb Mount Everest, the famous words of the British climber George Mallory were, "Because it is there." Unfortunately, to this day we do not know if George Mallory and his partner Andrew Irvine made it to the top when they tried to climb Everest in 1924. They died in the **attempt**, and it was only recently—in 1999—that Mallory's body was found on the mountain. People were sad about Mallory and Irvine's disappearance, and that is when the **fascination with** Everest began. There are many reasons why people climb mountains, such as personal satisfaction, **prestige**, power, the difficulty, and the **risk**, but they may also do it to understand their **inner strength**. The first man we can name who climbed a mountain for no reason other than that it was there was Frenchman Jean Buridan in the early fourteenth century.

2 Mount Everest, the highest mountain in the world, was named after Sir George Everest, a British surveyor in India who recorded the mountain's location in 1841. Mount Everest is in the Himalaya Mountains on the border of Nepal and Tibet. Its official height, which was determined by using a Global Positioning System satellite in 1999, is 29,035 feet (8,850 meters). Until then, every time surveyors measured the mountain, there was a difference of several feet. It was later found that the changing depth of ice at the **summit**, and not a mistake of the surveyors, was altering the mountain's height.

3 Many people had tried to climb Everest, but none were successful until 1953, when Edmund Hillary (later Sir Edmund Hillary) and Tenzing Norgay reached its summit. Edmund Hillary was from New Zealand, and Tenzing Norgay was a native Sherpa from Nepal. The Sherpas are skilled mountain climbers, and many of them are today's guides and porters in the expeditions to Everest.

4 Since 1953, many Everest records have been set by climbers who have tried the **unprecedented**. Ed Viesturs reached the summit without using extra oxygen. Junko Tabei was the first woman to reach the summit, and Lydia Bradley was the first woman to reach it without using extra oxygen. People with disabilities such as a blind man, a man with one arm, and a man with one leg also have reached the mountaintop. In 2003, a seventy-year-old man became the oldest person to reach the summit, and in 2010, a thirteen-year-old boy became the youngest person to get to the top. People have skied and snowboarded from the summit, three brothers reached it on the same day, and one person climbed Everest to sleep there. He slept for 21 hours! Speed records for the climb also have been set. The most recent one was 10 hours, 56 minutes.

(continued)

5   Needless to say, with all these attempts there have been many accidents and deaths on Everest. A blizzard in May 1996 killed eight climbers in one day. These climbers were in the best **physical condition** and had laptop computers, satellite phones, and other advanced equipment to help them climb the mountain. We know that sixty people died in the 1990s alone. In fact, one of every thirty climbers attempting to reach the summit has died, and yet climbers continue to risk their lives.

6   Today Everest has lost some of its old **mystique** and **appeal** because so many people are reaching its top. Thousands of mountaineers pass through base camp every year, but don't go as far as the summit. Close to 2,000 climbers have reached the summit, coming by every possible route. On May 16, 2002, 54 climbers reached the top successfully on the same day! These days, climbing Mount Everest has become a **novelty** for those who are in good physical condition and can afford to pay as much as $65,000 for climbing guides and fees. There are only a few months in the year that weather conditions make it practical to climb the mountain. These are April, May, October, December, and January. As a result, people usually have to make plans **in advance** to climb Everest. At one point, there was a twelve-year wait! It looks like the highest mountain in the world is becoming quite crowded. On the mountain, there is usually a line of people **waiting their turn** to get to the top. Even Sir Edmund Hillary was not **pleased with** the crowds. He said that if he were younger, he would not want to be in an expedition with so many people around.

7   Communication has always been a problem in such a remote area as Nepal. The telephones nearest to base camp, which is at 17,000 feet (5,182 meters), are a four-day walk away. These days, most trekkers (people who go on long and difficult walks) use satellite phones to run Web sites to contact their friends and family at home. Recently, someone had a better idea. A Sherpa, the grandson of a man from Nepal who was in the first expedition fifty years ago, plans to make an Internet café at the base camp of Everest. This will be the highest Internet café in the world! He is waiting for permission from the government to **go ahead with** the project. The money from the café will go to a project to clean up the tons of garbage left behind by the tens of thousands of tourists that come to Nepal every year.

8   Each of these tourists has his or her own reasons for climbing Everest. For many, the more **challenging** the mountain, the more they like it. These people know they risk their lives, but they don't mind. However, for many extreme climbers today, reaching the top of Mount Everest is not the challenge it once was, because too many people have done it. Many climbers want to go where no one has **dared**. Though it may be true that Mount Everest has lost some of its mystique, it is still the highest mountain on Earth. For this reason, it will probably always attract many of the world's best climbers.

VOCABULARY

MEANING

Circle the letter of the answer that is closest in meaning to the underlined word.

1. It was later found that the changing depth of ice at the <u>summit</u> was altering the mountain's height.
    a. bottom
    b. top
    c. middle
    d. end

2. Today, Everest has lost some of its old <u>mystique</u>.
    a. quality that makes something special
    b. quality that makes something dangerous
    c. quality that makes something popular
    d. quality that makes something beautiful

3. For many, the more <u>challenging</u> the mountain, the more they like it.
    a. difficult
    b. distant
    c. mysterious
    d. large

4. There are many reasons why people climb mountains, such as <u>prestige</u>, power, and the difficulty.
    a. happiness
    b. satisfaction
    c. fame
    d. health

5. Since 1953, many Everest records have been set by climbers who have tried the <u>unprecedented</u>.
    a. actions that are very dangerous
    b. actions that require strength to do
    c. actions that have never been done before
    d. actions that other people have done in the past

(continued)

6. Today, Everest has lost some of its old <u>appeal</u>.

    a. beauty

    b. difficulty

    c. danger

    d. interest

7. Many climbers want to go where no one has <u>dared</u>.

    a. been scared to go

    b. been brave enough to go

    c. wanted to go

    d. had the desire to go

8. There are many reasons why people climb mountains, such as the power, difficulty, and <u>risk</u>.

    a. enjoyment

    b. danger

    c. reward

    d. excitement

9. These days, climbing Mount Everest has become a <u>novelty</u>.

    a. something beautiful and charming

    b. something difficult and dangerous

    c. something big and costly

    d. something new and unusual

10. Mallory and Irvine died in the <u>attempt</u>.

    a. experience

    b. emotion

    c. effort

    d. climb

WORDS THAT GO TOGETHER

A. *Find words in the reading that go together with the words below to make phrases.*

    1. _____ their turn

    2. _____ ahead _____

3. fascination _____

4. physical _____

5. _____ strength

6. pleased _____

7. _____ advance

B. *Complete the sentences with the phrases from Part A.*

1. To have a _____ something is to have a powerful interest in it.
2. To be _____ something is to be satisfied and happy with it.
3. When people are _____, they can't do something because there are people in front of them who have to do it first.
4. The health and strength of your body, whether good or bad, is your _____.
5. To act _____ is to prepare for something before it happens.
6. When you _____ something, you begin or continue it.
7. Your bravery, courage, and mental ability to overcome pain and fear are all part of your _____.

C. *Now use the phrases in your own sentences.*

EXAMPLE: *People who eat healthy foods and exercise every day are usually in good* physical condition.

USE

Work with a partner to answer the questions. Use complete sentences.

1. What are two things that you usually need to do *in advance* when you go on a trip?
2. What are two types of accomplishments that bring people *prestige*?
3. Where can you often see people *waiting their turn*?
4. What is a place that has *mystique* for many people?
5. Where would you likely see people in excellent *physical condition*?
6. What are two sports that involve some *risk*?
7. What activity is physically *challenging*?
8. What famous place has an *appeal* to you?

COMPREHENSION

UNDERSTANDING MAIN IDEAS

Circle the letter of the best answer.

1. Paragraph 4 is mainly about how _____.
   a. a seventy-year-old man became the oldest person to reach the summit of Everest
   b. people have skied and snowboarded from the summit
   c. climbers have set many different records on Mount Everest
   d. people with disabilities have reached the summit

2. The main idea of paragraph 5 is that _____.
   a. over the years, there have been many accidents and deaths on Everest
   b. in 1996, eight climbers were killed in one day, even though they had computers and phones with them
   c. sixty people died on Everest in the 1990s alone
   d. one in every thirty climbers attempting to reach the summit of Mount Everest has died

3. The main idea of paragraph 6 is that _____.
   a. climbing Mount Everest has become a novelty for those who are in good physical condition and can afford to pay for guides and fees
   b. there are only a few months in the year that weather conditions make it practical to climb Mount Everest
   c. climbing Mount Everest has become so popular that the crowded mountain is losing some of its appeal
   d. Sir Edmund Hillary is not pleased with the crowds on Mount Everest

4. The main idea of paragraph 7 is _____.
   a. the nearest phones from the base camp are a four-day walk away
   b. many trekkers use satellite phones to contact their friends and family
   c. the money from an Internet café would go to a project to clean up tons of garbage left behind by climbers on Mount Everest
   d. a Sherpa plans to solve the communication problem on Everest by opening an Internet café

REMEMBERING DETAILS

Reread the passage and fill in the blanks.

1. The months in which weather conditions allow people to climb Everest are

   _____, _____, _____, _____, and

   _____.

2. The first man known to climb a mountain for no reason was _____, in the

   _____.

3. The first woman to reach the summit of Mount Everest was _____.

4. The official height of Everest is _____; it was determined by using a

   _____ in 1999.

5. Mount Everest is located in the _____ on the border of _____

   and _____.

6. The number of climbers who have reached the summit of Everest is _____.

7. The base camp of Mount Everest is located at a height of _____.

8. Edmund Hillary was a climber from _____, while Tenzing Norgay was a

   _____ from _____.

MAKING INFERENCES

The answers to these questions can be inferred, or guessed, from the reading. Circle the letter of the best answer.

1. The reading implies that Mallory and Irvine _____.
   a. couldn't have made it to the top of Everest
   b. didn't try to make it to the summit of Everest
   c. may possibly have made it to the top of Everest
   d. tried to climb Everest for scientific reasons

2. It can be inferred from the reading that _____.
   a. most climbers can make it to the summit of Everest without the help of guides
   b. most climbers need extra oxygen to make it to the summit of Everest
   c. most climbers can climb to the summit without extra oxygen
   d. only young people in top physical condition can make it to the summit

(continued)

3. From the reading, it can be concluded that _____.
   a. even with the help of modern technology, climbing Everest is still dangerous
   b. because of modern technology, climbing Everest is no longer dangerous
   c. fewer people are killed or hurt on Everest now than in the 1950s
   d. the weather isn't a cause in the accidents and deaths on Everest

4. The reading implies that _____.
   a. most people who climb Everest have been climbing mountains all their lives
   b. even inexperienced climbers can reach the summit of Everest
   c. most people are not willing to wait years to climb Everest
   d. though many people try to climb Everest, few make it to the summit

5. It can be inferred from the reading that _____.
   a. climbers on Everest have no way to contact people at home
   b. an Internet café on Everest will probably never be used
   c. climbers on Everest aren't interested in what Sir Edmund Hillary did in 1953
   d. the number of climbers on Everest is causing some problems with the environment

DISCUSSION

Discuss the answers to these questions with your classmates.

1. Would you like to climb Mount Everest? Why or why not?
2. What are some places in your country where people go to challenge themselves?
3. Why are more people doing dangerous activities now than ever before?
4. Is building an Internet café on Everest is a good idea? Why or why not?

CRITICAL THINKING

Work with a partner. Ask each other the following questions. Discuss your answers.

1. Imagine that you are about to climb Mount Everest. How are you feeling right now? What hardships do you expect? What physical and psychological challenges will you have to overcome to reach the summit? How do you think your physical and emotional states will change from day to day? How will you feel when you reach the summit? How will you feel when you go back to your normal life again?

2. What happens when areas of great scenic beauty and historical interest become popular with tourists? What changes must be made to accommodate the tourists? What kind of impact do tourists have on natural areas and ancient cities and monuments? What should be done to protect these places? Should tourists be allowed to visit them? Why or why not? How can we protect these areas for future generations?

WRITING

On separate paper, write a paragraph or an essay about one of the following topics.

1. What is the greatest challenge in your life? Why is it a challenge? What would you do once you faced or overcame the challenge?
2. What accomplishments have you had or would you like to have? Explain.
3. What is your favorite sport? Give two or three reasons.

GRAMMAR AND PUNCTUATION

THE DEFINITE ARTICLE: GEOGRAPHICAL NAMES AND DIRECTIONS

1. We use the definite article (*the*) with:

- groups of geographical features, such as mountain ranges, lakes, and islands, but not with the names of most single features. We <u>do</u> use *the* with names of single rivers and oceans.
  the *Himalayas,* **the** *Great Lakes* BUT *Mount Everest, Lake Superior;* **the** *Ganges River,* **the** *Pacific Ocean*

- plural names of countries, but not singular names of countries.
  the *United States,* **the** *Philippines* BUT *Japan, Canada*

2. For directions on the compass, we say:
  the *north of India* BUT *northern India*

We also say *the* Middle East and *the* Far East, but we use directions without *the* in names of some countries and regions:
  North America, South Africa

(Note: In most maps, *the* is <u>not</u> included in names.)

(continued)

Rewrite the incorrect sentences. Write the *where necessary.*

1. Africa's highest mountain is the Kilimanjaro.

   _____

2. Kilimanjaro is in the eastern Africa.

   _____

3. Himalayas are in north of India.

   _____

4. The Andros Island is the largest in the Bahamas.

   _____

5. Nile River flows from Lake Victoria in the Uganda into Mediterranean Sea in Egypt.

   _____

6. The Mount Blanc is the highest mountain in Alps.

   _____

7. The Rockies is the name of a mountain range in the west of the North America.

   _____

8. Hebrides Islands are in Atlantic Ocean along the western Scotland.

   _____

9. The Andes Mountains and Amazon River are both found in the South America.

   _____

10. Philippines is in Far East.

    _____

Go to page 171 for the Internet Activity.

DID YOU KNOW?

- The snowfields of the Himalayas never melt, not even in the summer.
- The Himalayas are still growing at a rate of 2.4 inches a year.
- The first skier to descend from the top of Everest was Davo Karnicar of Slovenia in 2000. It took him 5 hours.

Why Is the Renaissance Important?

you read

Answer these questions.

1. Who are some great artists in your country's past or present?

2. Who are some famous writers?

3. Who are some famous scientists?

WHY IS THE RENAISSANCE IMPORTANT?

1   During the period of the Middle Ages (from about 500 C.E. to the mid–1400s) there were few great changes in the **way of life** in Europe. People did what their fathers did before them, and there were few new inventions or discoveries. Most people believed in what they were told and did not care about anything outside of their lives. One reason for this may be because only a few people received an education, and books were scarce. Then, a change began. People became better educated, trade and industry developed, the arts **flourished**, and explorers discovered new lands. We call this great change the *Renaissance*, which in French means "rebirth." Many living at the time believed that the culture of ancient Greece and Rome had been reborn. The Renaissance, which took place in Europe between the thirteenth and sixteenth centuries, was a new **stage** in the history of the world.

2   Some people think that the Renaissance started when the Turks took over the Greek city of Constantinople (now Istanbul) in 1453. Greek scholars left Constantinople and settled in other parts of Europe. In these new locations, they taught Greek and shared their precious books. The study of classical Greek and Roman writers and thinkers became increasingly popular, and a new desire for learning spread throughout Europe.

3   People began to inquire into everything, and some began to question their beliefs and ways of thinking. In Germany, Martin Luther started a revolt against the **conventions** of the Roman Catholic Church. Soon, other Christians agreed that the Church needed to change, and several new Christian religions were established.

4   Other people began to think about new types of government that were based on the democratic values of ancient Greece. Italy, the birthplace of the Renaissance, was organized into city-states that governed themselves. Though wealthy families and the Church held much of the power in these areas, the city-states were moving a step **in the direction of** government by the people. The most famous political thinker of the Renaissance was Machiavelli. In his book on government, entitled *The Prince*, he stated that a good leader could do bad and dishonest things in order to **maintain** his power and protect his government. Though people in his own time thought that Machiavelli was evil for saying these things, his book is now famous, and modern political thinkers respect some of his ideas.

5   The "new learning" taught people to think in new ways, and it also **encouraged** gifted people to paint pictures, make statues and buildings, and write great literature. In fact, some of the best artists of the day did all of these things. As a

result, when a person today is skilled in many areas, he or she is often called a "Renaissance man" or a "Renaissance woman."

6   Many of the artistic developments of the Renaissance first happened in the Italian city of Florence, and then they spread to other Italian cities. **As a result of** trade and banking, cities such as Florence, Venice, and Milan became very wealthy, and their rich citizens had both the time and money to enjoy music, art, and poetry. These cities produced great painters and sculptors, such as Michelangelo, Leonardo, and Raphael. These artists created some of history's finest **works of art**. For example, Michelangelo spent four years painting the ceiling of the Vatican's Sistine Chapel. To do this, he had to paint lying on his back beneath the ceiling as paint dripped down onto his face. Despite these **obstacles**, he created one of art's greatest masterpieces.

7   A new kind of architecture also began in the Renaissance. It **blended** the old, classical styles with new ideas. Again, it started in Florence. The cathedral there had been started in 1296, but it remained unfinished for over 100 years because no one could figure out how to build the curved dome that it needed. Then, the architect Brunelleschi invented a new type of dome that was higher and grander than any from the classical **era**. The dome **marks** the beginning of Renaissance architecture.

8   From Italy, interest in the arts and new ways of thinking spread to other countries. Many painters in the north were influenced by the Italians; England produced many writers, including Shakespeare; and Spain had the literature of Cervantes. The new **passion for** learning also led to amazing discoveries in science by Vesalius, Harvey, Gilbert, Galileo, and Kepler. Some of these findings went against the most basic beliefs of the time. For example, Galileo's belief that the sun, not the Earth, was the center of the solar system got him into serious trouble with many religious people. They forced him to say that he had been wrong, even though he knew he was right.

9   The development of the printing press in Germany by a man named Gutenberg helped more than anything to spread the new ideas of the Renaissance. Before that time, books were scarce and very expensive because they were written by hand. Gutenberg discovered how to use a moveable metal type, and his first book was published in the 1450s. Printing was a very important invention. With it, books were made more cheaply and quickly than ever. In addition, most books had been written in Latin before, as this was thought to be the language of study. However, with the Renaissance, the middle classes could now afford books, and they wanted books in their own languages. They also wanted a greater variety of things to read, such as books on travel, poetry, and romance. Printing helped make the works of the best writers and all kinds of knowledge available to everyone.

10   About the time printing was invented, sailors were **setting out** on voyages of discovery. Now that the Turks were masters of the eastern Mediterranean, it was no longer possible to trade with India by the old land route. A new way had to be found, perhaps by sailing around the coast of Africa—or perhaps by sailing around the world! There were many explorers around this time, including Columbus, da Gama,

(continued)

Cabot, Magellan, and Drake. Representing countries throughout Europe, these men sailed new waters and discovered new lands, including the Americas. With all this travel, tools for exploration and navigation improved, and better ships were made. As people traveled, they gained new ideas that helped to change their way of living. For example, Europeans now wanted goods—such as spices, silk, and gold—from far away countries.

11   The Renaissance didn't begin suddenly when Constantinople was taken over by the Turks or when the first book was printed in the 1450s. Forces that **brought** it **about** had been developing for many years as Europeans began to desire and gain new knowledge. From this new learning came the great changes that we call the Renaissance. These advancements—from the invention of printing to a renewed interest in art and literature and the discovery of new lands—**affected** almost every area of European life. They also formed the basis for many parts of our modern life and beliefs. This is why some people think of the Renaissance as the beginning of modern history.

Vocabulary

MEANING

Circle the letter of the answer that is closest in meaning to the underlined word.

1. Martin Luther started a revolt against the <u>conventions</u> of the Roman Catholic Church.
   a. writings
   b. leaders
   c. speeches
   d. customs

2. Despite these <u>obstacles</u>, he created one of art's greatest masterpieces.
   a. methods
   b. changes
   c. difficulties
   d. differences

3. It <u>blended</u> the old, classical styles with new ideas.
   a. mixed together
   b. took apart
   c. put side by side
   d. put one over the other

4. The Renaissance was a new <u>stage</u> in the history of the world.
   a. special event
   b. long period of time
   c. step in development
   d. type of belief

5. The dome <u>marks</u> the beginning of Renaissance architecture.
   a. makes a statement about
   b. serves as a sign of
   c. gives an example of
   d. tells a story about

6. During the Renaissance, the arts <u>flourished</u>.
   a. grew and improved
   b. were almost forgotten
   c. were not accepted
   d. stayed about the same

7. In his book on government, entitled *The Prince*, Machiavelli stated that a good leader could do bad and dishonest things in order to <u>maintain</u> his power.
   a. put out of sight of others
   b. keep safe and unchanged
   c. make larger and stronger
   d. take away from

8. Brunelleschi invented a new type of dome that was higher and grander than any from the classical <u>era</u>.
   a. a particular area of the world
   b. a period in history
   c. a certain style of art
   d. a certain group of people

9. These advancements <u>affected</u> almost every area of European life.
   a. created
   b. defeated
   c. built up
   d. changed

10. The "new learning" <u>encouraged</u> gifted people to paint pictures.
    a. honored by important people
    b. ordered to change
    c. helped to become confident
    d. warned about other people

WORDS THAT GO TOGETHER

A. *Find words in the reading that go together with the words below to make phrases.*

1. _____ of art
2. way of _____
3. setting _____
4. _____ a result _____
5. brought . . . _____
6. passion _____
7. _____ the direction _____

(continued)

B. *Complete the sentences with the phrases from Part A.*

1. When you have strong and deep feelings for something, you have a _____ it.

2. When something happens because of an action or event, it happens _____ it.

3. _____ are objects that are produced by painting, writing, sculpting, and other creative skills.

4. If you are on a course toward something, you are moving _____ it.

5. The normal experiences and activities of a group or culture are its _____.

6. If something caused an event to happen, then that thing _____ the event _____.

7. If you are beginning a trip, you are _____ on a journey.

C. *Now use the phrases in your own sentences.*

EXAMPLE: As a result of *the bad weather, we had to cancel our hiking trip.*

USE

Work with a partner to answer the questions. Use complete sentences.

1. What are two of your favorite *works of art*?
2. When was the last time you *encouraged* someone to do something?
3. How is the *way of life* in your country different from that in another place you've been to?
4. What is a historical event that greatly *affected* the people in your country?
5. If you were *setting out* on a journey, where would you like to be going?
6. What part of nature would you like to *maintain* for future generations?
7. What is your favorite *era* in history?
8. Who is a historical figure that overcame many *obstacles* in his or her life?

COMPREHENSION

UNDERSTANDING MAIN IDEAS

Some of the following statements are main ideas and some are supporting statements. Some of them are stated directly in the reading. Find the statements. Write M for each main idea. Write S for each supporting statement.

_____ **1.** During the Middle Ages few people received an education and books were scarce.

_____ **2.** Most people believed in what they were told and did not care for anything outside their lives.

_____ **3.** People began to question their beliefs and ways of thinking.

_____ **4.** The most famous political thinker of the Renaissance was Niccolò Machiavelli.

_____ **5.** Many of the artistic developments of the Renaissance first happened in the Italian city of Florence, and then they spread to other Italian cities.

_____ **6.** Advancements in the Renaissance also formed the basis for many parts of our modern life and beliefs.

REMEMBERING DETAILS

Reread the passage and answer the questions. Write complete sentences.

1. What did Michelangelo spend four years painting?

_____

2. Who are three Renaissance scientists who made great discoveries?

_____

3. Who developed the printing press, and what country was he from?

_____

4. Who were five famous explorers of the Renaissance?

_____

5. What does the word *Renaissance* mean, and what language is it from?

_____

6. What does it mean when a person today is called a "Renaissance man" or a "Renaissance woman"?

_____

(continued)

7. What is the name of the architect who invented a new type of dome, and where was the cathedral for which he designed this dome?

_____

8. In what language had most books been written before the Renaissance?

_____

MAKING INFERENCES

The answers to these questions can be inferred, or guessed, from the reading. Circle the letter of the best answer.

1. The reading implies that before the Renaissance, _____.
   a. people were eager to learn new things
   b. education was limited to scholars and privileged people
   c. people wanted to change their lives but couldn't
   d. middle-class people did a lot of reading

2. From the reading, it can be concluded that the Renaissance _____.
   a. made people afraid to go against traditional beliefs
   b. influenced people to fight against each other
   c. helped leaders to maintain control over the middle class
   d. caused people to make changes in their lives

3. The reading implies that during the Renaissance, _____.
   a. economic prosperity was important to the development of the arts
   b. people were poor, but they still appreciated their artists
   c. there were many artists, but their works were not enjoyed by most people
   d. Italy was the only country that encouraged artists to produce new styles of art

4. It can be inferred from the reading that the major causes of the Renaissance were _____.
   a. explorations of new lands
   b. new artists and writers who created great works
   c. reading and learning
   d. changes in government

DISCUSSION

Discuss the answers to these questions with your classmates.

1. What do you think are the three most important inventions in the history of the world?
2. What do you think was the greatest period in the history of your country? Why?
3. Are art and literature important in modern society? Why or why not?

CRITICAL THINKING

Work with a partner. Ask each other the following questions. Discuss your answers.

1. Why is education important? In what ways does education change an individual, a society, and a country? How do the uneducated suffer? Why might an individual or group in power want to deny education to all or some of the people?
2. Compare our modern time with the Renaissance. In what ways are they similar? In what ways are they different? How are advances in technology, science, and medicine changing the world today? Are all of these changes good? Why or why not?

WRITING

On separate paper, write a paragraph or an essay about one of the following topics.

1. What is an invention that you think is important in your life? Give three reasons why it is important.
2. How have methods of study and learning changed in the last ten years? Are these methods better than those in the past? Why or why not?
3. What is one advancement in the field of medicine or science that has changed people's lives? State three ways it has helped people.

GRAMMAR AND PUNCTUATION

SHOWING CONTRAST: *THOUGH, ALTHOUGH; DESPITE, IN SPITE OF*

1. To show contrast or an unexpected result, we can use *though* or *although* to begin a subordinate (adverb) clause. The subordinate clause can come before or after the main clause; the meaning is the same. (*Though* is less formal than *although*.)

(continued)

> *Although* people once thought Machiavelli was evil for saying these things, his book is now respected by political thinkers.
> Machiavelli's book is now respected by political thinkers, *though* people once thought he was evil for saying these things.
>
> 2. We can also use the prepositions *despite* and *in spite of* to express contrast. They are followed by a noun.
> *Despite* these obstacles, Michelangelo created one of art's greatest masterpieces.
> *In spite of* these obstacles, Michelangelo created one of art's greatest masterpieces.

A. *Using the contrast word or phrase in parentheses, write a new sentence similar to the phrases and sentences below.*

1. China was more advanced; the Renaissance began in Europe. (*although*)

   _____

2. Galileo's belief that the sun was the center of the universe. He said he was wrong. (*despite*)

   _____

3. Most people think El Greco was Spanish. He was Greek. (*though*)

   _____

4. Our association of the Renaissance with art / Explorers and scientists were also a part of the Renaissance. (*in spite of*)

   _____

B. *Now write three sentences of your own using a contrast word or phrase.*

1. _____
2. _____
3. _____

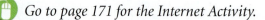 *Go to page 171 for the Internet Activity.*

Go to page 171 for the Internet Activity.

| **DID YOU KNOW?** | • During the Renaissance, Italy consisted of 250 separate states, most of which were ruled by a city.
• The Mona Lisa doesn't have any eyebrows because it was the fashion at the time to shave them.
• The Sistine Chapel is named after Pope Sixtus IV, who was responsible for building it. | |

WHAT IS THE MOST POPULAR SPORT IN THE WORLD?

you read

before

Answer these questions.

1. What is the most popular sport in your country?
2. What sports do you like? Which do you play?
3. Who are some famous sports stars of the past and present?

What Is the Most Popular Sport in the World?

1   Soccer—which is called *football* in most places—is the world's most popular sport. It is played in parks, fields, schools, and streets all over the world. It has about 250 million male and female players in more than 200 countries, and it has even more fans. In fact, billions of people around the world watched the 2006 World Cup tournament, making it the world's most watched television **sporting event**—it even **surpasses** the Olympics.

2   The exact origins of modern soccer are unknown. However, records show that the Chinese and Japanese played similar games over 2,000 years ago. Later, the ancient Greeks and Romans played it. The Romans took the game to Britain, which became the undisputed birthplace of modern soccer.

3   In Britain, the game came to be called *football*, because only the players' feet could touch the ball. However, when the British played football, it was more like war than a game. Towns and villages played against each other, and sometimes up to 500 people played on each team. There were even annual contests where large groups ran wildly from village to village playing the game. One game could last all day. Naturally, many people died and were injured. Several kings **banned** the game, passing laws against the sport because it was so rough and because soldiers preferred to play it rather than **concentrate on** military training. Even Queen Elizabeth I had players in London put into jail because they caused so much damage to shops and **public property** when they played in the streets. But the game was too popular to be stopped.

4   Football was played in many English schools as early as the 1800s, but it had no formal rules. Later, two sets of rules were developed. One set was **devised** at a school called Rugby, where players could handle and run with the ball. The game of rugby developed from these rules. Other schools preferred the hands-free game. In 1848, the general rules of the hands-free game were established at Cambridge University.

5   The Football Association of England was formed in 1863. At that time, university students created slang by adding -*er* to words they shortened. The name *soccer* developed from adding -*er* to the letters *s*, *o*, and *c* from the word *association*. However, the game is still known as football in most parts of the world **besides** North America, where *soccer* is more commonly used. Football quickly became popular throughout Europe and South America, and in 1900, it became one of the first **team sports** played in the Olympic Games. In 1904, seven nations—Belgium, Spain, Sweden, France, the Netherlands, Denmark, and Switzerland—met in Paris to form FIFA, the Fédération Internationale de Football Association. FIFA has been

the governing body of the sport **ever since**. Today, it has 204 member countries. Every four years, the world's strongest national football teams compete to be world champions and to get the World Cup—a golden trophy. The World Cup started in 1930. Beginning in 1958, it was held **alternately** in Europe and the Americas, but it was held in the United States in 1994, in 2002, Japan and South Korea and in South Africa in 2010.

6   Traditionally, football had been a game for male players, but now it has become popular with female players. Though women played football in China about 2,000 years ago, this was not heard of again until the game reappeared in the country's **school curriculum** for girls in the 1920s. **Appropriately**, the first Women's World Cup was held in China in 1991.

7   Throughout history, football was considered unsuitable for women in Europe, and they were banned from playing it. However, in the 1970s, women were allowed to play again, and the sport's popularity started to grow. Certainly, this **trend** will continue. Since 1996, women's football has been included in the Olympic Games, and today more than 7 million young girls play in the United States alone. The United States is a newcomer to the women's game, but has won the World Cup twice and has also won two Olympic gold medals and one silver medal. Players on the American team were the first women players to be paid as full-time professionals, but now other countries are following their lead. Though salaries are over $100,000 a year for the top female professionals, they are nowhere near the average of $5 million that their male **counterparts** make.

8   Every country thinks it has the best football team, but they all admit that Brazil is the world's greatest football-playing country. The sport was first introduced to Brazil by a British man named Charles Miller, who started a team there. In 1899, they played Brazil's first recorded game of football. Today, football is a way of life in Brazil. The Brazilian team was the first team to win the World Cup five times, and it has more professional teams than any other country in the world. Its talented players, such as Pelé, Garrincha, Zico, Ronaldo, Ronaldinho, and many others, have made Brazil famous throughout the world. These players **started out** very poor and became incredibly wealthy. They became true idols. Their influence can be seen on the young boys in the streets of poor neighborhoods throughout Brazil. The dream of most boys growing up in poverty there is to become a professional football player. It seems to be their only way to escape from poverty, and thus this sport has a greater influence on their lives than almost anything else.

9   Brazil is not the only country with football stars. Britain's David Beckham has become an idol for many young people. They read magazines about him and wait for his latest hairstyle to copy. In Tokyo, a giant, nearly 10-foot (3 meters) statue of Beckham made **entirely** of chocolate was made to **promote** a new kind of chocolate. Advertisers use him to sell many things, and of course, he makes millions of dollars from each advertising contract.

(continued)

10   Football is the one of the oldest sports in the world. It has been gaining fans across the globe for over 2,000 years, and it doesn't show any signs of stopping. Will football continue to be the most popular sport in the world? Most people think it will!

Vocabulary

MEANING

Circle the letter of the answer that is closest in meaning to the underlined word.

1. One set of rules was <u>devised</u> at a school called Rugby.
   - **a.** made up
   - **b.** thrown out
   - **c.** agreed to
   - **d.** added to

2. Beginning in 1958, the World Cup was held <u>alternately</u> in Europe and the Americas.
   - **a.** at the same time
   - **b.** once only
   - **c.** happening one after the other
   - **d.** every two years

3. It even <u>surpasses</u> the Olympics.
   - **a.** goes beyond
   - **b.** stays about the same as
   - **c.** is less than
   - **d.** becomes a part of

4. Female players' salaries are nowhere near the average of $5 million that their male <u>counterparts</u> make.
   - **a.** those in a different position
   - **b.** those in the same position
   - **c.** those in a lower position
   - **d.** those in a higher position

5. A giant statue of Beckham was made to <u>promote</u> a new kind of choco late.
   - **a.** stop the use of
   - **b.** create a new use for
   - **c.** prepare the way for
   - **d.** help the success of

6. Certainly, this <u>trend</u> will continue.
   - **a.** change of plan or action
   - **b.** general course or direction
   - **c.** new arrangement or idea
   - **d.** special place or situation

7. Several kings <u>banned</u> the game.

    a. tried to support   **c.** said to stop

    b. liked to play   **d.** believed in

8. A giant statue of Beckham was made <u>entirely</u> of chocolate.

    a. partly   **c.** evenly

    b. carefully   **d.** completely

9. The game is still known as *football* in most parts of the world <u>besides</u> North America.

    a. except   **c.** especially

    b. within   **d.** close to

10. <u>Appropriately</u>, the first Women's World Cup was held in China in 1991.

    a. correctly   **c.** accidentally

    b. wrongly   **d.** happily

WORDS THAT GO TOGETHER

A. *Find words in the reading that go together with the words below to make phrases.*

1. _____ curriculum

2. sporting _____

3. started _____

4. concentrate _____

5. _____ sports

6. ever _____

7. _____ property

B. *Complete the sentences with the phrases from Part A.*

1. Games played by groups of people are _____.

2. Something owned by a whole population is _____.

3. The courses offered in a school is the _____.

4. If you _____ in a certain manner, you began in that way.

5. A single sports contest among others is a _____.

6. _____ is the time between a point in the past and now.

7. If you _____ something, you keep all your attention on it.

(continued)

C. *Now use the phrases in your own sentences.*

EXAMPLE: *Some people would rather play individual sports than* team sports.

USE

Work with a partner to answer the questions. Use complete sentences.

1. *Ever since* the beginning of the Olympics, what have athletes dreamed of doing?
2. What is a place in your city or town that is *public property*?
3. What is the last *sporting event* that you watched, either on television or in person?
4. In your country, what is the latest fashion *trend*?
5. What are three *team sports* that are played in the summer Olympics?
6. What is something that the law in your country has *banned*?
7. What three areas of study are in most students' *school curriculum*?
8. What are examples of these three types of objects: one made *entirely* of wood, one of glass, and one of metal?

COMPREHENSION

UNDERSTANDING MAIN IDEAS

Look at the reading to find the answers to the following questions.

1. What is paragraph 2 mainly about?

   _____

2. Which sentence contains the main idea of paragraph 3?

   _____

3. Which sentence contains the main idea of paragraph 6?

   _____

4. What importance does Brazil have in the world of football?

   _____

5. What significance does David Beckham have to football fans?

   _____

REMEMBERING DETAILS

Reread the passage and circle the letter of the best answer.

1. Football was introduced to Brazil by _____.
   a. Pelé
   b. Garrincha
   c. Miller
   d. Zico

2. A giant chocolate statue of Beckham was made in _____.
   a. London
   b. Paris
   c. Tokyo
   d. Athens

3. In Britain, several kings banned football because _____.
   a. people were having too much fun
   b. too many people were getting killed and injured
   c. too many shops were being damaged
   d. it nearly started a war

4. The first Women's World Cup was held in _____.
   a. China
   b. Britain
   c. Brazil
   d. Japan

5. The hands-free game rules were established _____.
   a. at Cambridge University
   b. at a school called Rugby
   c. by the FIFA in Paris
   d. by the Football Association of England

(continued)

6. Football is usually NOT played in _____.

    a. fields

    b. parks

    c. streets

    d. courts

7. The first women football players to be paid as full-time professionals were _____.

    a. French

    b. American

    c. Brazilian

    d. Nigerian

8. In ancient times, the _____ took the game of football to Britain.

    a. Chinese

    b. Japanese

    c. Greeks

    d. Romans

MAKING INFERENCES

Some of the following statements are facts from the reading. Other statements can be inferred, or guessed. Write F *for each factual statement. Write* I *for of each inference.*

_____ **1.** At any time during the day or night, someone somewhere in the world is probably playing football.

_____ **2.** Britain is the undisputed birthplace of modern football.

_____ **3.** Although football was played in British schools in the 1800s, there were no formal rules to the game.

_____ **4.** Once game rules were established in Britain, it didn't take long for football to become a favorite sport around the world.

_____ **5.** In 1904, seven nations got together in Paris to form an international football association.

_____ **6.** Women played football in China as far back as 2,000 years ago.

_____ **7.** Football is a good way for the poor in Brazil to improve their lives.

_____ **8.** A popular football player can make as much or more money off the field as on it.

_____ **9.** Football is not the kind of sport that only appeals to a few people.

_____ **10.** Most people think that football will continue to be the most popular sport in the world.

DISCUSSION

Discuss the answers to these questions with your classmates.

1. Would you rather watch football or play it? Why?
2. Do you think that it's fair that women are paid so much less than men in professional sports? Why or why not?
3. Do professional athletes have a responsibility to be good role models, or examples, for young people? Why or why not? Are today's athletes good role models?

CRITICAL THINKING

Work with a partner. Ask each other the following questions. Discuss your answers.

1. In modern society, the idols of youth are actors, musicians, and sports figures. Why is this? What are the good and bad points of making idols of people in these fields? Are there other people in society that young people should look up to? Who has the most influence on your life?
2. What is the importance of sports in your country? What is the importance of sports in your own life? What role do sports play in the world? What do sports contribute to society? Do sports have any negative aspects in the world today?

WRITING

On separate paper, write a paragraph or an essay about one of the following topics.

1. Are the Olympic Games today good / bad / fair / important?
2. Should professional athletes participate in the Olympics? Explain your reasons.
3. Are the salaries of professional athletes too high? Why or why not?

GRAMMAR AND PUNCTUATION

THE DEFINITE ARTICLE: NATIONALITIES AND UNIQUE NOUNS

1. We can use the definite article *the* + nationality adjectives to mean "the people of a country." This is true for nationality adjectives that end in *-ch, -sh,* or *-ese* and function as nouns.
   *When **the British** played football, it was more like war than a game.*
   ***The Chinese** played football over 2,000 years ago.*

(continued)

(Note: We also use *the Swiss* to mean the people of Switzerland.)

With other nationalities, the plural noun ends in -s. We do not usually use *the* to talk about the people of these countries. However, we do use *the* when referring to ancient nationalities ending in *-s*.
Brazilians *love football.*
The *ancient* **Greeks** *and* **Romans** *played football.*

2. We use *the* when there is only one of a person, place, or thing. These are called unique nouns.
Football is the most popular sport in **the world**. *(There is only one world.)*

We therefore use *the* in front of superlatives such as *most* and *best*, and before *first, last, next, only, same, right,* and *wrong.*
Every country thinks it has **the best** *football team.*

Fill in the blanks with the *or* X *(for no definite article).*

1. Football was one of _____ first team sports played in _____ Olympics.

2. Some people think football is _____ oldest sport in history.

3. _____ Brazilians have some of _____ FIFA's most talented football players.

4. _____ French and _____ Swiss love football.

5. Today, football is not Japan's most popular sport, although _____ Japanese played it a long time ago.

6. _____ first full-time female professional players were _____ Americans.

7. _____ U.S. women's football team has won three Olympic medals.

8. Most people think Brazil is _____ greatest football-playing country in _____ world.

9. It was _____ Romans who introduced football to _____ British.

10. Brazil is _____ only country that has won _____ World Cup five times, and it also has had some of _____ most famous players.

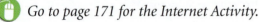 *Go to page 171 for the Internet Activity.*

| DID YOU KNOW? | • Soccer is the world's most watched and played, and biggest money making sport, and the second is cricket!
• In North America about 28% of soccer players are women!
• Europe has the largest number of soccer players in the world and has the world's richest and best known teams. |

HOW DID CONVICTS HELP SETTLE AUSTRALIA?

before you read

Answer these questions.

1. How many people do you think live in Australia today?

2. What are some famous places in Australia?

3. Would you like to visit Australia? Why or why not?

How Did Convicts Help Settle Australia?

1   The British were not the first Europeans to arrive in Australia. Dutch explorers had visited the vast continent before them. When an Englishman, William Dampier, landed in what is today New South Wales, he **condemned** the land as barren and useless. Then the British explorer Captain James Cook proved his **predecessor** wrong. He landed at Botany Bay in New South Wales in 1770, and with his botanist, Joseph Banks, he proved that the eastern shores were rich and fertile. Although Captain Cook gave an excellent report on the land he had seen in Australia, the British government made no effort to form a settlement there for several years.

2   For many years it was the **policy** of the British government to send men and women found guilty of breaking the law to America. There, as punishment, these prisoners were forced to work on big farms until they had **served out their sentences**, and they were then **set free**. This policy of sending criminals abroad was called "transportation."

3   However, all this changed with the loss of the American colonies. In 1776, the American colonies declared their independence from Britain. When they became the United States of America, no more **convicts** could be sent there. The British government was in a difficult position. People were still being sentenced to transportation, but there was nowhere to send them. Soon, the jails were overcrowded.

4   Joseph Banks, Captain Cook's botanist, suggested New South Wales as a good place for a convict settlement. "The soil is good there," he said, "and soon they will grow all their own food." Lord Sydney—after whom the capital of Australia is named—had the **task** of looking after the British colonies. He decided to try Banks's plan. He selected Captain Arthur Phillip, a naval officer, to take charge of the new settlement.

5   In May 1787, the First Fleet, consisting of eleven ships, left England for New South Wales. **On board** were about 1,400 people, of whom 780 were convicts. The rest were mainly soldiers to guard the convicts and seamen to work on the ships. About 20 percent of the convicts were women; the oldest convict was eighty-two, and the youngest was about ten years old. The voyage to Australia was very slow. It took eight months; six of these were spent at sea, and two were spent in ports to get supplies. The fleet finally arrived in Botany Bay in 1788. Two more convict fleets arrived in 1790 and 1791, and ships continued to come to other ports in Australia for over seventy years.

6   A major problem of the convict system was the **severity** of its punishments. Among the convicts on the First Fleet was a woman who was transported for stealing a coat. The British also transported a man who had received a sentence of fourteen years for killing a rabbit on his master's property. Others were transported only because they supported different political opinions. There were many real criminals who were transported as well, but **by today's standards**, few of the convicts would be considered criminals.

7   Conditions on the ships were **deplorable**. Ship owners were paid "per head," or for each person they transported. To make as much money as possible, the owners overcrowded the ships. The convicts were chained below deck, where there was no sunlight or fresh air. They suffered a lot, and many died on the way. Because so many died on the ships, the government later paid a bonus to ship owners whose passengers had arrived **safe and sound** at the end of the journey.

8   For convicts who **made it** to Australia, conditions were a little better. Those who were well behaved were **assigned to** settlers as workers or servants, and if they worked for good people, they served out their sentences under pleasant conditions. Other convicts worked in groups for the government. They did various kinds of jobs, such as clearing land, making roads and bridges, and constructing public buildings. Those convicts who refused to work or tried to escape were severely punished.

9   Convicts could win their freedom back more quickly with good behavior. They could qualify for a "Ticket of Leave" or a "Certificate of Freedom." Convicts who got their freedom were allowed to move around the country and work in any kind of profession they liked. Soon, many educated ex-convicts became lawyers, teachers, and business owners. Others bought land and became rich settlers.

10   Convicts were not the only settlers in the country; free settlers had been coming from Britain and starting farms since 1793. In the beginning, the convicts were a great help to the new settlers. But later, when the number of free settlers grew, they objected to the transportation of convicts. They thought it was unfair that their new land was filled with criminals. By 1840, objection was so strong that no more convicts were transported to the mainland. Instead, they were sent to Tasmania, an island south of Australia.

11   Convicts had never been sent to western Australia, but in the middle of the nineteenth century, the colony there suddenly asked for them. There was a shortage of **labor** in the region, and the colony could only progress with convict labor. Britain supplied the colony with convicts starting in 1850 and ending in 1868, and the convicts helped build it up by constructing roads, bridges, and public buildings.

12   A total of 162,000 men and women—transported on 806 ships—came as convicts to Australia. By the time the British policy of transportation ended, the population of Australia had increased to over a million. Without the convicts' hard work, first as servants and later as settlers, it wouldn't have been possible for the government and

(continued)

the free settlers to create a nation. The transportation of convicts is an essential part of Australia's history. Today, many Australians **acknowledge** their convict ancestors and are **grateful** for their contributions to the country.

VOCABULARY

MEANING

Circle the letter of the answer that is closest in meaning to the underlined word.

1. No more <u>convicts</u> could be sent to the American colonies.
   a. colonists
   b. prisoners
   c. soldiers
   d. government officials

2. Conditions on the ships were <u>deplorable</u>.
   a. enjoyable
   b. terrible
   c. surprising
   d. depressing

3. There was a shortage of <u>labor</u> in the region.
   a. farmers
   b. settlers
   c. workers
   d. business owners

4. Many Australians are <u>grateful</u> for the contributions of their convict ancestors.
   a. thankful
   b. ashamed
   c. lucky
   d. punished

5. He <u>condemned</u> the land as barren and useless.
   a. described
   b. disapproved of
   c. announced
   d. gave a name to

6. Today, many Australians <u>acknowledge</u> their convict ancestors.
   a. try to hide the facts about
   b. remember the details of
   c. admit the truth about
   d. tell a story about

7. It was the <u>policy</u> of the British government to send men and women found guilty of breaking the law to America.
   a. belief
   b. problem
   c. demand
   d. way of doing things

8. A major problem of the convict system was the <u>severity</u> of its punishments.

    a. lightness   **c.** popularity

    b. strangeness   **d.** seriousness

9. Captain James Cook proved his <u>predecessor</u> wrong.

    a. someone who came before   **c.** someone who arrived at the same time

    b. someone who left after   **d.** someone who would come in the future

10. Lord Sydney had the <u>task</u> of looking after the British colonies.

    a. thought   **c.** job

    b. plan   **d.** choice

WORDS THAT GO TOGETHER

A. *Find words in the reading that go together with the words below to make phrases.*

1. _____ board

2. made _____

3. served _____ their _____

4. _____ and sound

5. assigned _____

6. set _____

7. by _____ standards

B. *Complete the sentences with the phrases from Part A.*

1. Convicts who have completed all the time of their punishments in jail have

_____.

2. When a person is _____ someone, the person is given to him or her to use.

3. People who are riding on a bus, train, plane, or ship are _____ that form of transportation.

4. People who are _____ are allowed to go out and act as they want, and are no longer under someone else's control.

5. If you are _____, you are alive, not in danger, and in good health.

(continued)

6. If you arrive somewhere, you can say that you have _____ there.

7. Many legal penalties from the past seem harsh _____.

C. *Now use the phrases in your own sentences.*

EXAMPLE: *The search party looked for the hiker, and after two days, they found him* safe and sound.

USE

Work with a partner to answer the questions. Use complete sentences.

1. What is a *policy* in your school or workplace that you don't agree with? Explain why.

2. What is a *task* that you must do at work or home?

3. What is a place that has *deplorable* conditions? Describe it.

4. If you could be *on board* any form of transportation right now, how would you like to be traveling? Where would you be going?

5. What is something that you are *grateful* for?

6. What are three types of *labor* that are important to your country's economy?

7. If you were suddenly *set free* from your school, job, and other obligations, what is the first thing you would do?

8. What are two things that people are often afraid to *acknowledge*?

COMPREHENSION

UNDERSTANDING MAIN IDEAS

Circle the letter of the best answer.

1. The main idea of paragraph 1 is that _____.
    a. the explorer Dampier condemned New South Wales as a barren and useless land
    b. the British formed a settlement many years after Captain Cook arrived in Australia
    c. explorers from many countries visited Australia before the British finally started a settlement there
    d. Captain Cook and his botanist, Joseph Banks, proved that the eastern shores of New South Wales were rich and fertile

2. The main idea of paragraph 5 is that _____.
   a. on board the First Fleet were about 1,400 people, of whom 780 were convicts
   b. of the eight months it took the First Fleet to get to Australia; six were spent at sea and two at port getting supplies
   c. about 20 percent of the convicts were women; the oldest convict was eighty-two, and the youngest about ten
   d. over seventy years of convict transport began in 1787, when the First Fleet of convicts, soldiers, and seamen sailed to Australia

3. The main idea of paragraph 10 is that _____.
   a. the first free settlers came in 1793 and started farms
   b. in the beginning, the convicts were a great help to the free settlers
   c. free settlers finally stopped the transportation of convicts to Australia
   d. after 1840, convicts were transported to the island of Tasmania

4. The main idea of the last paragraph is that _____.
   a. 162,000 men and women—transported on 806 ships—came as convicts to Australia
   b. today many Australians acknowledge their convict ancestors
   c. by the time the British policy of transportation ended, the population of Australia had grown to over a million
   d. the convicts played an important part in the history of Australia

REMEMBERING DETAILS

Reread the passage and answer the questions. Write complete sentences.

1. Why was one of the convicts on the First Fleet given a sentence of fourteen years?

   _____

2. Why did the free settlers object to the transportation of convicts?

   _____

3. When and where did Captain James Cook arrive in Australia?

   _____

4. Who was the first British official to decide to send convicts to Australia?

   _____

(continued)

5. Why did many of the convicts suffer and die on the first voyages to Australia?

   _____

6. How many ships were in the First Fleet?

   _____

7. What are three jobs that the convicts did for the government in Australia?

   _____

8. When did the last shipment of convicts arrive in Australia?

   _____

MAKING INFERENCES

Some of the following statements are facts from the reading. Other statements can be inferred, or guessed. Write F for each factual statement. Write I for each inference.

_____ 1. Even though Cook told the British government how good the land was, they didn't make any effort to settle Australia for several years.

_____ 2. The convict settlement of Australia probably wouldn't have happened if the American colonies hadn't declared their independence.

_____ 3. Though the voyage was extremely difficult, the convicts were better off in Australia than in England's crowded jails.

_____ 4. Ship owners were paid "per head," or for each person they transported.

_____ 5. The ship owners had little caring or compassion for the convicts.

_____ 6. As free settlers increased, they objected to having convicts in their new land.

_____ 7. The convicts had valuable skills and knowledge.

_____ 8. In western Australia, the convicts constructed roads, bridges, and public buildings.

DISCUSSION

Discuss the answers to these questions with your classmates.

1. What do you think about the British sending their convicts to Australia? Would this type of "transportation system" work today? Why or why not?

2. Should convicts today do hard work such as building roads?

3. Is your country an "old" country or a "new" country? What are the advantages and disadvantages of living in an ancient land? In a new land?

4. Would you like to explore a new country? Why or why not?

CRITICAL THINKING

Work with a partner. Ask each other the following questions. Discuss your answers.

1. What are some of the immigration problems facing countries today? Should countries have open borders, closed borders, or controlled immigration? Why? What is the immigration policy in your country? Why are some people against immigration?

2. Many of the convicts sent to Australia became good citizens and some went on to do important things in government and business. Can criminals be rehabilitated, that is, trained to live a good and normal life? Why or why not? Should criminals only be punished in prison or should they be allowed to play sports and have training and education? Should life in prison be the maximum sentence for the worst crimes?

WRITING

On separate paper, write a paragraph or an essay about one of the following topics.

1. What are some problems you may encounter when you live in a new country?

2. Describe or explain the fairness of the justice system in relation to some crimes we hear about in the news. Are court decisions generally fair or unfair?

3. What should the punishment be for minor crimes (such as driving too fast or taking something from a supermarket without paying)?

GRAMMAR AND PUNCTUATION

THE PAST PERFECT

To form the past perfect, we use *had* + the past participle of the verb. Notice the past perfect verb in the second sentence below.

> *The British were not the first Europeans to arrive in Australia. Dutch explorers **had visited** the vast continent before them without giving it much notice.*

Had visited is the past perfect of the verb *visit*. The past perfect shows that something happened before another past event or time. In this case, first the Dutch visited the continent. Then the British arrived in Australia.

(continued)

Read the sentences from the reading. Identify the order of events. Write 1 for the first event and 2 for the second event.

1. Although Cook gave an excellent report on all the land he had seen in Australia, the British government made no effort to form a settlement there for several years.

   _____ Cook gave an excellent report.

   _____ Cook saw all the land.

2. These convicts were forced to work on big farms until they had served out their sentences, and they were then set free.

   _____ Convicts served their sentences.

   _____ Convicts were set free.

3. Banks, a colleague of Cook who had been with him to Australia, suggested New South Wales as a good place for a convict settlement.

   _____ Banks suggested New South Wales as a convict settlement.

   _____ Banks was in Australia with Cook.

4. The British also transported a man who had received a sentence of fourteen years for killing a rabbit on his master's property.

   _____ The man received a sentence of fourteen years.

   _____ The British transported the man.

5. Because so many died on the ships, later the government paid a bonus to ship owners whose passengers had arrived safe and sound at the end of the journey.

   _____ The passengers arrived safe and sound.

   _____ The government paid a bonus to ship owners.

6. By the time the British policy of transportation ended, the population of Australia had increased to over a million.

   _____ The policy of transportation ended.

   _____ The population increased to over a million.

Go to page 172 for the Internet Activity.

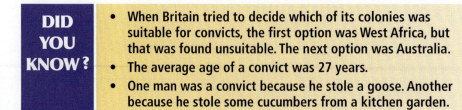

DID YOU KNOW?

- When Britain tried to decide which of its colonies was suitable for convicts, the first option was West Africa, but that was found unsuitable. The next option was Australia.
- The average age of a convict was 27 years.
- One man was a convict because he stole a goose. Another because he stole some cucumbers from a kitchen garden.

WHAT IS THE STORY OF TEA?

before you read

Answer these questions.

1. What are your favorite beverages?
2. What is the most popular beverage in your country?
3. What is the traditional way in which tea or coffee is served in your country?

WHAT IS THE STORY OF TEA?

1   Tea is the most popular beverage in the world, and there are many customs related to how it is made, served, and drunk. Some like it black, and some like it green. Some add milk and butter, while others add spice and sugar. Tea is poured into cups, bowls, and glasses. It is served for good health and **hospitality**. It is drunk at social events, formal ceremonies, and in bed. But no matter how, when, or why tea is served, it is a pleasure all around the world.

2   The history of tea goes back 5,000 years to ancient China. According to legend, the Chinese emperor Shen Nung was boiling water over an open fire, and some dried leaves from a nearby plant fell into it. The emperor drank it and found it **refreshing**. Soon all of China was enjoying tea. From China, tea was brought to Japan by a Buddhist monk. A few centuries later, tea drinking in Japan was raised to an art form in the Tea Ceremony. The Dutch brought tea from China to Europe in 1610. In the Netherlands, tea was a luxury and cost $100 a pound. Ladies from the best families had tea parties where they served each guest with cakes and 50 or more cups of tea! The first tea samples got to England between 1652 and 1654, where it became so popular that it soon replaced beer as England's national drink.

3   Today tea is drunk in every corner of the world. The Chinese drink their tea as they did centuries ago, and it has great importance in their society. They prefer green tea and always offer a bowl to guests. In some homes, a traditional Chinese tea ceremony is still performed, using an **earthenware** pot and delicate tea bowls. In almost every neighborhood and business district there are tea houses that attract large crowds. Tea houses are the center of Chinese **social life**.

4   As in China, green tea has a special place in Japanese culture and is always served to guests. Although the Japanese now enjoy many types of teas in their homes, cafés, and even British-style tea rooms, the traditional Tea Ceremony is still performed. It is an art that takes years of study and practice. The ceremony contains the four principles of Zen: harmony, respect, purity, and **tranquility**. It takes place in a tea house in a garden away from the main house and surrounded by a wall to separate it from the problems of the outside world. The visitors take a **winding** path to the house, which is made of wood and paper, a symbol that life is not lasting. The door to the tea room is low, so visitors have to bend as they enter, showing that everyone is equal. Everything about the ceremony is symbolic—the container with water that symbolizes purity, the tea bowl that represents the moon, and so on. The ceremony lasts about four hours, and each part of it is enjoyed in a special way. A true master makes the movements look natural and simple, and by the time everyone leaves, they have a feeling that they have been part of a poem.

5   Drinking tea is not as ceremonial in Great Britain, but tea still holds a high place in daily life. For the British, tea is the cure for a headache or a **heartache**. It seems anything can be fixed by a "nice cuppa tea." The British usually drink black tea

with milk and sometimes sugar. When tea was first brought to England, it was served in a bowl, but many had difficulty holding the bowl by the base and **rim** without burning their fingers, so they poured small amounts of tea into their saucers to cool. The ladies and gentlemen then picked up their saucers and **slurped up** the liquid! To avoid this, a single handle was added to the tea cup around the middle of the eighteenth century. The custom of slurping tea from saucers eventually stopped, but still continues in parts of England and India. Soon another custom was started by one of Queen Victoria's Ladies in Waiting, the Duchess of Bedford. At that time, the British had two meals a day, breakfast and dinner. During the long wait between meals the Duchess had a "sinking feeling," so she began to invite friends for an afternoon meal of small cakes, sandwiches, and tea. Other ladies liked the idea and started to do the same. Later, there were two kinds of afternoon teas: "low tea" and "high tea." High tea is served around five or six o'clock on a dining table (a high table) and is a rather large meal with hot dishes, heavy sandwiches, and cakes. Low tea is served around 4 P.M. and consists of light cakes and thin sandwiches without **crusts**.

6   Americans didn't drink a lot of tea. Americans **associated** tea **with** the British, with whom they fought the Revolutionary War, so they drank coffee instead. Today, Americans drink lots of tea, but about 80 percent of it is "iced." Iced tea was born in 1904 at the St. Louis World's Fair when an Englishman named Richard Blechynden wanted to **promote** Indian teas. His plan to serve samples of hot tea didn't **work out** so well. That day the temperature was extremely hot, and everyone wanted cold lemonade and Coca-Cola. Blechynden immediately **came up with** an idea: he filled tall glasses with ice cubes and poured hot tea over them. The beverage was an immediate **hit**. Shortly after iced tea was invented, the tea bag was born. An American tea salesman named Thomas Sullivan **gave away** samples of tea in small silk bags. His customers put them in a cup and poured hot water over them. People thought it was a great idea, and later tea bags were made of cheaper paper filters. Today tea is more popular than ever in America, particularly if it's conveniently available in bags, instant mixes, and bottles and cans—perfect for a society **on the go**.

7   Tea customs vary around the world. In Mongolia, tea is mixed with milk, butter, and grain—almost like a soup—and drunk from a bowl. Moroccans favor green tea, served with fresh mint and sugar in small glasses. Indians drink a spiced tea known as *chai*, made with hot milk, sugar, cinnamon, and cardamom.

8   No other beverage has such worldwide appeal. Tea soothes and refreshes, and in this busy world, gives us a moment to pause. For many, a morning without tea would be unthinkable. Not to offer tea to a guest would be rude. Tea holds a special position in our lives and traditions. It is so important that we can't even imagine what we would do without it.

VOCABULARY

MEANING

Circle the letter of the answer that is closest in meaning to the underlined word.

1. It is served for good health and <u>hospitality</u>.
   - **a.** taking care of a sick person
   - **b.** going places with other people
   - **c.** showing attention to guests
   - **d.** doing something pleasurable

2. The emperor drank it and found it <u>refreshing</u>.
   - **a.** producing a sense of tiredness
   - **b.** providing a feeling of extreme joy
   - **c.** giving comfort and strength
   - **d.** causing one to fall asleep right away

3. The traditional tea ceremony is still performed, using an <u>earthenware</u> pot.
   - **a.** vessels made of fine china
   - **b.** vessels made of baked clay
   - **c.** vessels made of wood
   - **d.** vessels made of metal

4. The ceremony contains the four principles of Zen: harmony, respect, purity, and <u>tranquility</u>.
   - **a.** quiet and peacefulness
   - **b.** laughter and joy
   - **c.** delight and pleasure
   - **d.** energy and activity

5. The visitors take a <u>winding</u> path.
   - **a.** turning one way and another
   - **b.** going in a straight direction
   - **c.** going around in a circle
   - **d.** rising up a hill

6. For the British, tea is the cure for a headache or a <u>heartache</u>.
   - **a.** violent feeling of anger
   - **b.** strong feeling of pleasure and joy
   - **c.** deep feeling of sorrow and pain
   - **d.** sharp feeling of disgrace and dishonor

7. Many had difficulty holding the bowl by the base and <u>rim</u> without burning their fingers.
   - **a.** bottom
   - **b.** inside surface
   - **c.** front
   - **d.** top edge

8. "Low tea" consists of light cakes and thin sandwiches without <u>crusts</u>.
   - **a.** small pieces of pastry
   - **b.** meat on bread
   - **c.** the brown outside surface of baked bread
   - **d.** the light, soft inside part of bread

9. Richard Blechynden wanted to <u>promote</u> Indian teas.

    a. keep a secret of   **c.** make use of

    b. help the sale of   **d.** take interest away from

10. The beverage was an immediate <u>hit</u>.

    a. improvement   **c.** progress

    b. failure   **d.** success

WORDS THAT GO TOGETHER

A. *Find words in the reading that go together with the words below to make phrases.*

   1. _____ up _____

   2. on _____ go

   3. gave _____

   4. _____ life

   5. work _____

   6. slurped _____

   7. associated _____

B. *Complete the sentences with the phrases from Part A.*

   1. Things you do with other people are part of your _____.

   2. If you _____ your coffee, you drank it noisily.

   3. If you _____ a plan, you created it in your mind.

   4. If your plan does _____, it has a good result.

   5. When you are going somewhere and doing something every minute, you are

      _____.

   6. If something is _____ something else, it means that it is
connected to it in some way.

   7. You _____ something if you made a present of it.

C. *Now use the phrases in your own sentences.*

EXAMPLE: *I'm so tired because I was* on the go *all day today.*

(continued)

USE

Work with a partner to answer the questions. Use complete sentences.

1. What are some advantages of cooking and serving food and beverages in *earthenware* pots, cups, and bowls?
2. What may be left on the *rim* of a cup after a woman drinks from it?
3. What are some *hit* movies that you have seen?
4. What beverages do you find *refreshing*?
5. What are some ways in which companies *promote* their products?
6. What are some places in which there are *winding* paths?
7. What are some times in which people suffer from *heartache*?
8. What are some ways in which we show *hospitality*?

COMPREHENSION

UNDERSTANDING MAIN IDEAS

Circle the letter of the best answer.

1. The main idea of paragraph 2 is that tea _____.
   a. started in China
   b. quickly became popular in Britain
   c. was a luxury in the Netherlands
   d. spread from China to Japan and Europe

2. Paragraph 4 is mainly about _____.
   a. the different parts of the tea ceremony
   b. the type of tea the Japanese prefer
   c. how a tea house is made and why
   d. how people feel about the tea ceremony

3. Paragraph 5 is mainly about _____.
   a. why tea is so important to the British
   b. the ways in which tea has been served in Britain
   c. why a tea cup with a handle began to be used
   d. how "high tea" and "low tea" got started

4. The main idea of paragraph 6 is that in America, _____.

   a. iced tea was born at the St. Louis World's Fair

   b. tea became popular after iced tea and bagged tea were invented

   c. people didn't drink tea because they associated it with the British

   d. people like tea that is in bottles and cans

REMEMBERING DETAILS

Reread the passage and fill in the blanks.

1. Tea was brought from China to Japan by a _____.

2. Between the years _____, the first tea was brought to Great Britain.

3. A Japanese tea house is built away from the main house and surrounded by a wall because the owner wants to _____.

4. The door to a tea room is made low because _____.

5. "High tea" is served around _____ on a high table with a _____ meal.

6. Hot tea was not working well at the World's Fair because _____.

7. People in Mongolia like their tea mixed with _____.

8. The _____ drink a spiced tea called *chai*.

MAKING INFERENCES

Some of the following statements can be inferred from the reading and others cannot. Circle the number of each statement that can be inferred.

1. In the 1600s, the Dutch were trading goods with China.

2. In the early 1600s, only the wealthy could enjoy tea in the Netherlands.

3. The Chinese have no place else to meet except tea houses.

4. Anyone can master the art of the Japanese tea ceremony.

5. The tea ceremony is meant to refresh the spirit as well as the body.

6. Tea is more than just a beverage to the British.

7. Americans like things that go with their busy lifestyle.

8. Most likely, tea will not be so popular in the future.

DISCUSSION

Discuss the answers to these questions with your classmates.

1. What are some health benefits of green tea? Which is better for you, tea or coffee? Why? Are large amounts of either drink good for a person? Why or why not?

2. Why do you think people take such pleasure in drinking a cup of tea or coffee? What is the most popular time for people to drink these beverages? What are some famous coffee shops around the world? Why do people like to go to coffee shops even though they can make their own coffee at home?

CRITICAL THINKING

Work with a partner. Ask each other the following questions. Discuss your answers.

1. Many cultures have developed ceremonies around the drinking of tea or coffee. Is there such a ceremony in your country? If so, describe it. What are some of the purposes of these ceremonies?

2. Explain how each of the principles of Zen—harmony, respect, purity, and tranquility—are important in family life and in society as a whole. Why are these principles still as important to modern society as they were thousands of years ago?

WRITING

On separate paper, write a paragraph or an essay about one of the following topics.

1. Write about table manners in my country.
2. Write about tea / coffee customs in my country.
3. Write about what a guest or a host should do in my country.

GRAMMAR AND PUNCTUATION

FORMS OF *OTHER*

We use forms of *other* as adjectives or pronouns to mean "more things or people of the same kind."

- *Another* means one more in addition to the one we already have talked about.
  *Soon **another** custom was started by one of Queen Victoria's Ladies in Waiting. (= one more custom)*

- *Other* or *others* (without *the*) means several more in addition to the one(s) we already talked about.

> **Other** ladies liked the idea and started to do the same.
>
> Of the various tea ceremonies, the Japanese is more complex than **others**.

- *The other* or *the others* means all that is remaining from a specific group. (Note: *the others* is often used with *all* or *all of*.)

  *There are two popular kinds of tea in the U.S.: one is herbal tea and **the other** is iced tea.*

  *Tea as a beverage is more popular than **all the others**.*

- *Each other* and *one another* are reciprocal pronouns. *Each other* usually refers to two subjects and *one another* to more than two; however, we use either of the two forms in informal English.

  *Indian tea and Moroccan tea are different from **each other**.*

  *Teas in Asia are different from **one another**.*

Complete the sentences with a form of other *from the list below. You may use the words more than once.*

another	other	others	the other	the others	each other

1. Tea went from China to _____ countries.

2. After iced tea, Americans had _____ great idea—tea bags!

3. Strong, hot English tea and sweet, iced American tea are very different from

   _____.

4. Customs of tea drinking are different from one _____.

5. Some countries drink tea from glasses. _____ use bowls and cups.

6. They say green tea is healthier than _____.

7. There are two main kinds of tea: one is black and _____ is green.

8. When I finished my cup of tea, she asked me if I wanted _____ cup.

9. This tea was delicious! It was better than all _____ I had tasted.

10. Some teas were perfumes with flowers; _____ were smoky in aroma.

🖱️ *Go to page 172 for the Internet Activity.*

<table>
<tr><td>DID YOU KNOW?</td><td>
<ul>
<li>A cup of black tea has half the amount of caffeine in a cup of coffee.</li>
<li>In one day, an experienced tea picker can collect 70 pounds of tea. That's enough for 14,000 cups.</li>
<li>The Chinese word for tea is cha.</li>
<li>One tea plant can produce tea for 50 years.</li>
</ul>
</td></tr>
</table>

WHY IS ERNEST SHACKLETON'S EXPEDITION TO ANTARCTICA SO FAMOUS?

before you read

Answer these questions.

1. Where is Antarctica?
2. Say three things you know about Antarctica.
3. What are some problems you would face to survive there?
4. Imagine you were left there with no food or transportation. What would you do?

Why Is Ernest Shackleton's Expedition to Antarctica So Famous?

1   Antarctica surrounds the South Pole. It is covered by an ice sheet thousands of feet thick. Where the ice sheet meets the sea, huge pieces break off. They float away as icebergs. The waters around Antarctica are packed with ice most of the year. The weather is **severe**. In the late 1890s, the first explorers arrived in Antarctica. Eventually some tried to make it all the way to the South Pole. In 1901, Ernest Shackleton, an Englishman, joined an **expedition** to Antarctica, but no attempt was made to reach the pole. In 1911, Roald Amundsen of Norway reached it.

2   Three years later, Shackleton tried a new **challenge**. He wanted to cross the entire continent on foot. The **hardships** of that expedition—a true tale of survival—made him famous. In December 1914, Shackleton and his crew of twenty-eight men set sail for Antarctica on the *Endurance*. They left from South Georgia, a small island in the southern Atlantic. After six weeks, they were only a day's sail from Antarctica. Suddenly the ship became surrounded by ice. During the night a storm arose. It pushed the ice against the ship. The next morning the ice was solid around it. They were **trapped**! Spring was nine months away. All the crew could do was to wait. Meanwhile, blizzards hit them **night and day**. The temperatures were as low as 30 degrees below zero. Months passed. Finally, in October 1915, the ship started to crack. The men quickly removed their supplies and lifeboats. They set up camp on the ice. Eventually the ship sank. For the next five months the men stayed on the ice. In their tents, they were hit by storms. They **endured** temperatures far below freezing. Shackleton tried twice to march over the ice to land. But it was impossible to carry the tons of supplies and heavy wooden lifeboats. Meanwhile, they drifted on the ice toward open sea.

3   Finally the ice began to melt. On April 9, 1916, Shackleton ordered everyone into three lifeboats. They were **headed for** a tiny finger of land called Elephant Island. It was 100 miles away. They sailed and rowed for a week through wind, snow storms, and huge waves. More than once, the men almost lost their lives. Finally, they landed on Elephant Island. By this time, the men were very weak. Their clothing was ragged. They were ill and suffered from frostbite. They had almost no supplies left, and winter was coming. Blizzards constantly hit the island. They could not survive there for long.

4   Shackleton had the **fate** of his men in his hands. He had to give them hope. He was **faced with** a difficult decision. Courageously, he chose his five best sailors and the largest lifeboat. They would try to sail over 800 miles to the whaling station on

(continued)

South Georgia Island. Their prospects were not good. They had to cross the coldest and stormiest seas in the world. Shackleton left Frank Wild **in command** of the men on the island. Wild was a good leader. He helped the men to build shelters from the two remaining lifeboats. He sent out hunting parties to find food.

5   Meanwhile, Shackleton and his crew of five began the greatest boat journey in history. As they crossed the stormy seas, huge waves broke over the small boat. Water poured in. The men threw water over the side. Worse yet, ice began to form on the boat. Desperately, they chipped off the ice. More continued to form. The ice was dangerous on the mast[1] and rigging.[2] It made the boat too heavy on top. For five days the wind and waves struck them. Several times the boat almost turned over. Finally the sea calmed. They had survived! For three days, the men enjoyed the quiet seas. But once again the wind howled. Huge waves formed. The men battled for their lives. They were exhausted and thirsty. Their feet were numb from frostbite. The challenges to their survival were unimaginable. Nevertheless, after sixteen days, they landed on South Georgia Island. Unfortunately, a storm had pushed them into an uninhabited part of the island. Their journey and their trials were not over. Once again, Shackleton made a brave choice. After a brief rest, he and two men started a 22-mile hike over the snow-covered mountains. The interior of the island had never been mapped. They had to find their way **on their own**. They took some rope and a compass. They put screws from their boat on their worn shoes. It was bitter cold, and they had no tent and very little food. If they stopped, they would freeze. So they climbed and they walked without stopping for 36 hours. Finally they reached the whaling station. They were by now dressed **in rags**. They looked like walking ghosts. The manager of the station asked, "Who are you?" Shackleton introduced himself. Everyone had thought that Shackleton and his men were dead. They were alive! The whalers opened their arms to receive them. Then they rescued the men left behind on the other side of the island.

6   Next, Shackleton had to rescue his men on Elephant Island. He took a small whaling boat. Sixty miles from the island, ice and snow storms forced him back. Shackleton tried again. This time he had to stop within 18 miles. A third try also failed. After three months had passed, the government of Chile loaned him a strong boat. On August 30, 1916, they arrived at Elephant Island. Shackleton looked through his binoculars. He counted the men on the beach. What joy! All of his men had survived.

7   Shackleton's expedition was a failure. But in the end he did much more than walk across a continent. He and his men had been **stranded** in the world's most **hostile** environment. They had survived. Shackleton proved to be a great leader. He and his men had **persevered** through the greatest adversities. They had survived **against all odds**. Their two-year journey would become legend.

---

[1] **mast** = the tall upright pole that supports the sail
[2] **rigging** = the ropes that support the ship's mast and sails

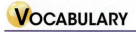

VOCABULARY

MEANING

Circle the letter of the answer that is closest in meaning to the underlined word.

1. The weather is <u>severe</u>.

   a. mild   **c.** steady

   b. harsh   **d.** heavy

2. Ernest Shackleton led an <u>expedition</u> to the South Pole.

   a. a trip made for no reason   **c.** a long journey, especially to a dangerous

   b. a long walk   place

                                     d. a social gathering

3. In 1914, Shackleton tried a new <u>challenge</u>.

   a. test   **c.** opportunity

   b. change   **d.** force

4. The <u>hardships</u> of that expedition made him famous.

   a. difficult conditions   **c.** large amounts of work

   b. great successes   **d.** long lengths of time

5. They were <u>trapped</u>!

   a. not able to speak   **c.** not able to live

   b. not able to breathe   **d.** not able to leave

6. They <u>endured</u> temperatures far below freezing.

   a. died from   **c.** took part in

   b. ran from   **d.** suffered through

7. Shackleton had the <u>fate</u> of his men in his hands.

   a. what a person has experienced   **c.** what will happen to a person

   b. what a person believes in   **d.** what a person needs or wants

8. He and his men had been <u>stranded</u>.

   a. forced to go to   **c.** sent away from

   b. left alone without help   **d.** asked to stay in

(continued)

9. They had been stranded in the world's most <u>hostile</u> environment.

    a. unfriendly   **c.** welcoming

    b. forgiving   **d.** disappointing

10. He and his men had <u>persevered</u>.

    a. given up   **c.** kept going

    b. complained about   **d.** stopped moving

WORDS THAT GO TOGETHER

A. *Find words in the reading that go together with the words below to make phrases.*

1. _____ command
2. _____ their _____
3. headed _____
4. _____ rags
5. faced _____
6. _____ all _____
7. night _____

B. *Complete the sentences with the phrases from Part A.*

1. You are _____ a decision when you are in a situation that you must do something about.

2. Something goes on _____ when it continues from one morning to the next.

3. A person who gives orders to others is _____.

4. When people do something without the help of others, they do it _____.

5. You are dressed _____ when your clothes are old and worn out.

6. When the chances are that something will not happen and then it does, it has happened _____.

7. If you are moving in the direction of something, you are _____ it.

C. *Now use the phrases in your own sentences.*

EXAMPLE: *The children made a snowman* on their own.

USE

Work with a partner to answer the questions. Use complete sentences.

1. What have you achieved because you *persevered*?
2. Where would it be better to be *stranded*, in a desert, ocean, or ice and snow?
3. What is the most *severe* weather that you have ever experienced?
4. What is the difference between being *trapped* and feeling trapped? Have you ever been or felt trapped? Explain.
5. What is the greatest *challenge* that you have faced, or are facing, in your life?
6. Before modern transportation, what *hardships* did early travelers experience?
7. What are two famous *expeditions* by early explorers?
8. What is the most *hostile* environment you have ever experienced?

COMPREHENSION

UNDERSTANDING MAIN IDEAS

Circle the letter of the best answer.

1. Paragraph 1 is mainly about _____.
   a. the location and weather in Antarctica
   b. Ernest Shackleton's expedition to the South Pole
   c. explorers who went to Antarctica
   d. Roald Amundsen's successful expedition in 1911

2. The main idea of paragraph 2 is that _____.
   a. Shackleton's ship wasn't strong enough to survive the ice
   b. the weather in Antarctica is severe and dangerous
   c. it was impossible for Shackleton to carry his supplies to land
   d. Shackleton and his men became dangerously trapped in ice

(continued)

3. The main idea of paragraph 3 is _____.

    a. the hardships suffered by Shackleton and his men

    b. the difficult decision Shackleton was faced with

    c. how Shackleton and his men got to Elephant Island

    d. how Frank Wild helped the men survive

4. Paragraph 4 is mainly about _____.

    a. how Shackleton and his crew battled waves and ice on the boat

    b. the dangers and challenges endured by Shackleton and his crew

    c. Shackleton's journey over snow-covered mountains

    d. the whalers' surprise upon seeing Shackleton and his men

REMEMBERING DETAILS

Reread the passage and fill in the blanks.

1. When pieces break off the ice sheets into the sea they become _____.

2. The ship became trapped in solid ice because _____.

3. The men had to sail _____ miles in their lifeboats to get to Elephant Island.

4. The men could not survive on Elephant Island for long because _____ and _____.

5. Frank Wild helped the men to _____, and he _____.

6. The ice on the mast and rigging was dangerous because _____.

7. Shackleton and his men took _____ and _____ to help them get over the mountains.

8. When Shackleton looked through his binoculars he _____.

MAKING INFERENCES

Some of the following statements are facts from the reading. Other statements can be inferred, or guessed. Write F for each factual statement. Write I for each inference.

_____ **1.** Antarctica is covered by an ice sheet thousands of feet thick.

_____ **2.** After Amundsen successfully reached the South Pole, Shackleton lost interest in going there himself.

_____ **3.** It took Shackleton six weeks to sail from South Georgia to Antarctica on the *Endurance*.

_____ **4.** After months trapped in the ice, the ship began to crack.

_____ **5.** If Shackleton had not left his men on Elephant Island, they all would have died.

_____ **6.** Frank Wild believed that Shackleton would save them.

_____ 7. The men never gave up their fight for survival.

_____ 8. Even after Shackleton arrived on South Georgia Island, their hardships were not over.

_____ 9. Shackleton refused to give up on rescuing his men.

_____ 10. Shackleton proved that he was a great leader.

DISCUSSION

Discuss the answers to these questions with your classmates.

1. What are some other places in the world where the environment is harsh and hostile? Why do you think people live in these places? What are some of the characteristics of the people who live there? Would you like to live in a remote or harsh area? Why or why not?

2. Would you like to join an expedition to a harsh and unknown place? Why or why not? What kind of people join such expeditions? What characteristics and qualities do you think they have?

3. What kept Shackleton and his men fighting for survival for eight months? What are some of the reasons why not a single man died during this expedition?

4. Do you think it is easier to survive alone or in a group? What are the advantages and disadvantages of being stranded alone and of being stranded with a group of people?

CRITICAL THINKING

Work with a partner. Ask each other the following questions. Discuss your answers.

1. Imagine you are stranded in the desert, on the ocean, in a jungle, and in the Arctic. What would you do to survive in each of these places? What place in the world do you think you'd actually enjoy being stranded in? Why?

2. There are leaders in many different areas, such as business, politics, sports, science, and exploration. What are the qualities of a good leader in each of these fields? In what ways are leaders in these fields alike? In what ways are they different? What makes a person a bad leader?

WRITING

On separate paper, write a paragraph or an essay about one of the following topics.

1. What are the advantages and/or disadvantages of living in a hot climate or a cold climate?

2. What are the advantages of perseverance?

3. Describe a difficult decision. Write about the positive side(s) and the negative side(s) of the situation and the decision you made and why.

GRAMMAR AND PUNCTUATION

PARALLEL STRUCTURE

> We use conjunctions such as *and*, *but*, and *or* to connect words or phrases. The words before and after these conjunctions must have the same grammatical form. This means there is parallel structure.
>
> The men quickly removed their **supplies** and **lifeboats**. (nouns)
> They had to cross the **coldest** and **stormiest** seas in the world. (adjectives)
> The storms came **quickly** and **violently**. (adverbs)
> They **sailed** and **rowed** for a week. (verbs)

Rewrite the incorrect sentences with correct parallel structure. Use correct word forms.

1. There were strong windy, snow storms, and huge waves.

   _____

2. The men suffered from frostbite and hungry.

   _____

3. Shackleton was a great explorer and leadership.

   _____

4. Shackleton was trying again and stopped within 18 miles.

   _____

5. His men had been stranded, and they have survived.

   _____

6. They had neither tents nor some food.

   _____

7. If they stopped, they could freeze and dead.

   _____

8. Once again, the wind howled and waves forming.

_____

9. He looked through his binoculars and count the men on the beach.

_____

10. They looked tired and weakness.

_____

 Go to page 173 for the Internet Activity.

Go to page 173 for the Internet Activity.

DID YOU KNOW?	• The cold and dry conditions of the Dry Valleys in Antarctica are close to conditions on the planet Mars. The Valleys are used by NASA. It has not rained in the valleys for 2 million years. • Antarctica has a special group of fish called ice fish. Their blood is clear and has no red color, which gives them a ghostly white color. • Only about 0.4 percent of Antarctica is not covered by ice.	

WHO INVENTED THE WORLD WIDE WEB?

Answer these questions.

1. Do you use a computer? If so, what do you mostly use it for?
2. What are the Internet and the World Wide Web used for?
3. How important are computers in society today? Why?

WHO INVENTED THE WORLD WIDE WEB?

1   Tim Berners-Lee is not a **household name** like Bill Gates. He is not **outrageously** rich or famous. He could have been, but he didn't want to be. Tim Berners-Lee is a quiet man who does not like the **spotlight**. He is the man who invented the World Wide Web and revolutionized the Internet. Berners-Lee's invention permits anyone with a computer to easily access a vast amount of information on any subject. This is a great **contribution to** the use of computers and to society. Some people believe it is as important as Gutenberg's printing press.

2   Tim Berners-Lee was born in London, England, in 1955. He grew up in a family that talked a lot about computers and math, since both of his parents were computer scientists who worked on the design of the first commercial computer. As a small child, he made computers out of cardboard boxes. Later, when he attended Oxford University to study physics, he made his first real computer. He constructed it out of various parts of a machine and an old television set. He graduated from Oxford in 1976, and in the next few years worked for several high-tech companies in England.

3   Around 1980, Berners-Lee was hired for a short period at the European Particle Physics Laboratory (CERN) in Geneva, Switzerland. It was there that he created a software program called *Enquire* that **linked** documents in the laboratory's information system. The purpose of this system was to **store** a vast amount of information that could be accessed in a very short **time span**. This was the basis for the tool he later created and named the World Wide Web.

4   Berners-Lee left CERN to work for another computer company for a few years. When he returned, he found that his Enquire program had been forgotten. He suggested to his employer that Enquire could be expanded with graphics, text, and video to work on a worldwide basis using the Internet, which had been invented in 1989. But CERN was not a company that could develop such a project. So Berners-Lee worked on his own and created the World Wide Web.

5   Many people think that the World Wide Web and the Internet are the same thing, but they **actually** are not. The Internet is like a large bridge that connects millions of computers around the world and makes it possible for them to communicate with each other. There are different ways to send and receive information over the Internet. These include e-mail, **instant messaging**, and, of course, the Web. Each of these ways uses a special set of rules that sends information over the bridge of the Internet.

(continued)

6 The World Wide Web went on the Internet in 1991. In the beginning, it only had 600,000 users, mostly people in education. But after a while, computer users understood the new **medium**. By 2002, it was estimated that some 600 million people worldwide were using the Web.

7 Undoubtedly, Berners-Lee must have **turned down** numerous offers with which he could have made a lot of money. But making money is not his goal. He is an idealist whose main **pursuit** is knowledge. In 1994, Berners-Lee joined the Laboratory for Computer Science at the Massachusetts Institute of Technology (M.I.T.). He has been working there quietly since, and his earnings as director are probably no more than $90,000 a year. He keeps a **low profile** and can walk the streets of his city unrecognized. He can devote time to his wife and two children.

8 By 1995, *Internet* and *World Wide Web* were familiar words. These inventions made a huge **impact on** modern business and communication. The Web has become a way for many businesses to sell themselves and their products. Many companies now include Web addresses on their business cards and in their advertising.

9 Now, some people think there are things on the Web that are **distasteful**. They want governments to keep this kind of material off of the Web. But Berners-Lee thinks the Web should not be **censored**. He said, "You don't go down the street, after all, picking up every piece of paper blowing in the breeze. If you find that a search engine gives you garbage, don't use it. If you don't like your paper, don't buy it." (*Technology Review*, 1996 July, pp. 32–40)

10 Berners-Lee *is* concerned about security on the Web. He suggests having an on-screen **icon** called *Oh, Yeah?* that can be used by someone who is unsure about something they see on the Web. For example, if someone was shopping online and wanted to make sure that they could trust a company, he or she could click on the icon to receive confirmation that it was safe.

11 Berners-Lee has received numerous awards for his work on the Web, including a knighthood in 2003 by Queen Elizabeth II for services to the global development of the Internet. This now makes him Sir Timothy Berners-Lee. Berners-Lee has fought hard to keep the World Wide Web open with no ownership, so it is free for all of us to use. We do not know how Berners-Lee will shape the future of the Web. He hopes the Web will become a tool for social change and wants to be a part of that development. The World Wide Web has already revolutionized the way the world learns; now Berners-Lee hopes it can make the world a better place to live.

VOCABULARY

MEANING

Circle the letter of the answer that is closest in meaning to the underlined word.

1. The purpose of this system was to <u>store</u> a vast amount of information.
   a. use
   b. create
   c. put together
   d. keep

2. After a while, computer users understood the new <u>medium</u>.
   a. machine used to send information
   b. way of communicating
   c. subject to study
   d. knowledge to complete a task

3. Berners-Lee thinks the Web should not be <u>censored</u>.
   a. examined for removal
   b. added to
   c. changed
   d. sold

4. Berners-Lee is a quiet man who does not like the <u>spotlight</u>.
   a. loud noise
   b. crowded areas
   c. a lot of attention
   d. lots of money

5. Some people think there are things on the Web that are <u>distasteful</u>.
   a. likeable
   b. complicated
   c. unpleasant
   d. incorrect

6. Berners-Lee created a software program called *Enquire* that <u>linked</u> documents.
   a. separated
   b. connected
   c. discovered
   d. saved

7. He is an idealist whose main <u>pursuit</u> is knowledge.
   a. effort
   b. problem
   c. fear
   d. idea

8. He is not <u>outrageously</u> rich or famous.
   a. outwardly
   b. unkindly
   c. understandably
   d. shockingly

(continued)

9. Many people think that the World Wide Web and the Internet are the same thing, but they <u>actually</u> are not.

   a. unbelievably   c. usually

   b. almost   d. truly

10. He suggests having an on-screen <u>icon</u> called *Oh, Yeah?*

    a. word   c. program

    b. picture   d. key

WORDS THAT GO TOGETHER

A. *Find words in the reading that go together with the words below to make phrases.*

1. impact _____

2. _____ messaging

3. contribution _____

4. _____ span

5. turned _____

6. _____ profile

7. _____ name

B. *Complete the sentences with the phrases from Part A.*

1. If you _____ something, you refused it.

2. _____ is a very fast way to communicate with someone over the Internet.

3. If someone is famous and everybody knows about him or her, then he or she is a _____.

4. If an object, idea, situation, or person has an effect on others, it has an _____ them.

5. A length of time over which something continues is a _____.

6. If you avoid drawing attention to yourself and your actions, you are keeping a _____.

7. If you are doing something to help others, you are making a _____ them or their cause.

C. *Now use the phrases in your own sentences.*

EXAMPLE: *I turned down the job offer because the pay was too low.*

USE

Work with a partner to answer the questions. Use complete sentences.

1. What are three important inventions of the twentieth century that had an *impact on* people's lives?
2. Who is *outrageously* rich or famous in your country?
3. What is *censored* in your country?
4. What kind of behavior do you find *distasteful*?
5. What person has made an important *contribution* to your happiness?
6. Who in your country is a *household name*?
7. What would you do if you had to keep a *low profile*?
8. Where in your home can you *store* things?

COMPREHENSION

UNDERSTANDING MAIN IDEAS

Circle the letter of the best answer.

1. Paragraph 2 is mostly about _____.
   a. where Berners-Lee grew up
   b. the influence of Berners-Lee's parents on his career
   c. Berners-Lee's achievements at Oxford
   d. Berners-Lee's earliest efforts with computers

2. Paragraph 5 is mostly about how the Internet _____.
   a. is like a bridge
   b. works
   c. is different from the Web
   d. uses special rules

(continued)

3. The main idea of paragraph 8 is that _____.
   a. the *Internet* and *World Wide Web* are familiar words
   b. businesses use the Web to sell themselves and their products
   c. the Internet and the World Wide Web have made a big impact on business and communication
   d. companies include Web addresses on their business cards and advertising

4. Paragraph 10 is mainly about how _____.
   a. Berners-Lee wants to have an on-screen icon called *Oh, Yeah*?
   b. Berners-Lee wants to improve security on the Web
   c. an online shopper might not trust a company
   d. people can't shop safely on the Web

REMEMBERING DETAILS

Reread the passage and answer the questions. Write complete sentences.

1. How many users did the World Wide Web have at the beginning, and who were they?
   _____

2. What kind of work did Berners-Lee's parents do?
   _____

3. What has Berners-Lee fought hard to do?
   _____

4. What do some people want governments to do on the Web?
   _____

5. What did the Enquire program do?
   _____

6. What are three different ways to transport information over the Internet?
   _____

7. Why did Queen Elizabeth II give Berners-Lee a knighthood?
   _____

8. What does the World Wide Web permit computer users to do?
   _____

MAKING INFERENCES

The answers to these questions can be inferred, or guessed, from the reading. Circle the letter of the best answer.

1. The reading implies that _____.
    a. Berners-Lee would like more people to acknowledge his great invention
    b. the World Wide Web is not as important as many people say it is
    c. the World Wide Web can be compared to the greatest inventions in history
    d. the World Wide Web had only a small effect on the Internet

2. From the reading, you can conclude that _____.
    a. Berners-Lee's parents were a bad influence on him
    b. Berners-Lee grew up poor
    c. Berners-Lee's childhood had a lot to do with his success
    d. Berners-Lee knew nothing about computers until he graduated from Oxford

3. From the reading, you can conclude that the World Wide Web was _____.
    a. not an immediate success
    b. a big success right after it was invented
    c. a disappointment to many people
    d. only for people in the field of computer science

4. From the reading, it can be concluded that Berners-Lee _____.
    a. knew from the beginning that his Enquire program would be used worldwide
    b. believes that work and family are more important than fame and fortune
    c. wishes he had never invented the World Wide Web
    d. thinks he has not received the money he deserves for his invention

5. The reading implies that Berners-Lee _____.
    a. is not interested in the future of the World Wide Web
    b. thinks people should continue using the Web even if they don't like it
    c. would like to see all harmful information taken off the Web
    d. wants his invention to be good for society

DISCUSSION

Discuss the answers to these questions with your classmates.

1. What are the positive and negative aspects of the World Wide Web?
2. How can the World Wide Web be used as a tool for social change? Is social change always a good thing? Why or why not?
3. How has the World Wide Web made the world a better place?
4. Should Berners-Lee have accepted fame and fortune? What is your opinion of the choices he has made in his life?

CRITICAL THINKING

Work with a partner. Ask each other the following questions. Discuss your answers.

1. An idealist is a person who pursues high or noble principles or goals. Do you know any idealists of the present or past? Who are they? Do you think it was easier to be an idealist in the past than it is today? Why or why not? What sacrifices does an idealist make? What benefits does an idealist enjoy?
2. Should people be more concerned about security on the Web? Why or why not? Who should worry the most about security? Should people do their banking and shopping online? What are the benefits? What are the dangers? Are personal networking sites such as Facebook and MySpace secure? Do people reveal too much about themselves on these sites? What are the advantages and disadvantages of social networking websites?

WRITING

On separate paper, write a paragraph or an essay about one of the following topics.

1. What are the advantages and/or disadvantages of using the Internet or the World Wide Web?
2. Should the World Wide Web be censored? Give reasons.
3. How has the World Wide Web changed the way people buy things?

THE DEFINITE ARTICLE: INVENTIONS AND THE MEDIA

1. Usually, *the* is not used with nouns that represent a general group or the idea of something. However, *the* <u>is</u> used when referring to an invention in general.
   He works with computers. BUT *He invented **the** computer.*

2. *The* has special uses in references to the media (ways of communicating). For example, when referring to the radio and television media, we say:
   *I listen to **the** radio a lot.* BUT *I watch a lot of television.*

   However, we do use *the* when talking about an actual television set.
   *I turned off **the** television and went to work.*

Fill in the blanks with the *or* X *(no definite article).*

1. _____ printing press is one of the world's most important inventions.

2. He put _____ television in his bedroom.

3. _____ computer has changed our lives.

4. When he was a child, his parents often talked about _____ computers.

5. _____ instant message may be the fastest way to communicate today.

6. The twentieth century brought amazing inventions in _____ technology.

7. Before _____ television, we had _____ radio.

8. _____ society is better today because of the Internet.

9. When was _____ computer invented?

10. Do you prefer to play computer games or to watch _____ television?

Go to page 173 for the Internet Activity.

DID YOU KNOW?

- The abbreviation WWW has three times as many syllables as the full term World Wide Web and takes longer to say—but it's easier to type.
- The word *google* is a misspelling of *googol*—a number that is 1 followed by one hundred zeros.
- The Web started as a tool to help physicists understand the universe.
- Today households want a computer to go on the web—not to compute.
- MySpace started in July, 2003. Today it has 100 million users.

SELF-TEST 2

Units 9–16

A. COMPREHENSION

Circle the letter of the correct answer.

1. The idea of the curse of King Tut began when _____.
   a. some people died after the discovery of Tut's tomb
   b. Carter brought a yellow canary to Egypt and it immediately died
   c. the Egyptians buried Tut in the Valley of the Kings and saw a cobra
   d. Carter and Carnarvon began to search for Tut's tomb and fell ill

2. Mount Everest _____.
   a. is no longer a difficult mountain to climb
   b. is no longer popular with climbers
   c. remains a mountain that few people have reached the top of
   d. is still a dangerous mountain to climb, although many people have succeeded

3. During the Renaissance, _____.
   a. people violently revolted against their governments and old ways of life
   b. there were few major changes except in the field of science
   c. people became interested in the arts for the first time in history
   d. people gained new knowledge and interests in the arts, sciences, and exploration

4. Modern football _____.
   a. began as a school game in Brazil and then spread around the world
   b. started as a woman's sport until it became a popular men's sport in Europe
   c. developed in Britain from a game without rules to a world-famous sport
   d. began to lose its popularity as it spread from Europe to South America and Asia

5. Convicts sent to Australia from Britain _____.
   a. made life difficult for the settlers there
   b. helped to build and create the nation
   c. died in great numbers from poor treatment
   d. eventually left Australia for new lives in the United States

6. In most countries around the world, tea _____.
   a. is only used for special ceremonies
   b. still has a special place in their culture and lifestyle
   c. has become only one of many quick and convenient beverages
   d. is served the same way it was served in ancient China

7. Shackleton's expedition to Antarctica became famous because _____.
   a. of the hardships and dangers they survived
   b. they successfully walked across the continent
   c. they were the first men to explore the continent
   d. they sailed there without losing their ship

8. Tim Berners-Lee invented the World Wide Web as a way to _____.
   a. communicate with other businesses
   b. become famous and earn a lot of money
   c. store a large amount of information
   d. link computers around the world

B. VOCABULARY

Complete the sentences. Circle the letter of the correct answer.

1. By 1935, there were twenty-one _____ of the curse.
   a. opportunities   b. displays   c. wounds   d. victims

2. Today, Mount Everest has lost the _____ it once had.
   a. priority   b. task   c. severity   d. appeal

3. During the Renaissance, the arts _____.
   a. encouraged   b. flourished   c. collapsed   d. dared

(continued)

4. Up to 1994, the World Cup was held _____ in Europe and the Americas, but since then it has been held in North America, Asia, and Africa.

    a. eventually   **b.** appropriately   **c.** actually   **d.** alternately

5. Conditions on the first ships transporting convicts to Australia were _____.

    a. deplorable   **b.** humiliated   **c.** distasteful   **d.** unprecedented

6. For the British, tea is the cure for a headache or a _____.

    a. rim   **b.** heartache   **c.** tranquility   **d.** hospitality

7. Shackleton and his men _____ very harsh conditions.

    a. required   **b.** presented   **c.** persevered   **d.** endured

8. We don't hear much about the man who invented the Web because he doesn't like the _____.

    a. pursuit   **b.** spotlight   **c.** summit   **d.** medium

C. GRAMMAR AND PUNCTUATION

Circle the letter of the sentence or sentences with the correct grammar and punctuation.

1.   **a.** Mummies were an Egyptian invention.

    b. The mummies were an Egyptian invention.

    c. Mummies were the Egyptian invention.

    d. Mummies were Egyptian invention.

2.   **a.** Mount Everest is in the Himalayas, a mountain range in the India, the Nepal, and the Tibet.

    b. Mount Everest is in the Himalayas, a mountain range in India, Nepal, and Tibet.

    c. The Mount Everest is in Himalayas, a mountain range in the India, Nepal, and Tibet.

    d. Mount Everest is in Himalayas, a mountain range in India, Nepal, and Tibet.

3.   **a.** The art of the Renaissance began in Florence although it spread to other cities.

    b. Although the art of the Renaissance spread to other cities, it began in Florence.

    c. The art of the Renaissance spread to other cities though it began in Florence.

    d. The art of the Renaissance spread to other cities. It began in Florence, although.

4. **a.** Football is the most popular sport in world.

   b. Football is most popular sport in world.

   c. Football is the most popular sport in the world.

   d. Football is most popular sport in the world.

5. **a.** The British government has shipped convicts to America until the settlement in New South Wales was established.

   b. The British government shipped convicts to America until the settlement in New South Wales is established.

   c. The British government had shipped convicts to America until the settlement in New South Wales was established.

   d. The British government had shipping convicts to America until the settlement in New South Wales was established.

6. **a.** Tea went from China to another countries.

   b. Tea went from China to others countries.

   c. Tea went from China to other countries.

   d. Tea went from China to the others countries.

7. **a.** They were hit with strong windy, snow storms, and huge waves.

   b. They were hit with strong winds, snow storms, and huge waves.

   c. They were hit with strong winds, snowing storms, and huge waves.

   d. They were hit with strong winds, snow stormy, and huge waves.

8. **a.** Tim Berners-Lee invented the World Wide Web, but not the computer.

   b. Tim Berners-Lee invented World Wide Web, but not computers.

   c. Tim Berners-Lee invented World Wide Web, but not the radio.

   d. Tim Berners-Lee invented World Wide Web, but not television.

APPENDICES

INTERNET ACTIVITIES

UNIT 1

1. Work in a small group. Use the Internet to learn more about life in Medieval times. Find the answers to three of these questions. Share your information with your classmates.

   1. How did people spend most of their time?
   2. What did they find at their village fairs?
   3. Who was educated and what subjects were they taught?
   4. What types of clothing were worn by the peasants, nobility, and knights?
   5. What types of games did people play?
   6. What kind of music was played and on what instruments?
   7. What were the customs of marriage and romance?

2. Use the Internet to find out about one of these fortifications. Find out what the fortification is, who built it, and where, when, and why it was built. Share your information with your classmates.
   Anastasian Wall, Babylon Fortress, Fort Jesus, Hadrian's Wall, Maginot Line, Mannerheim Line, the Alamo, Suomenlinna Fortress

UNIT 2

1. Work in a small group. Use the Internet to learn about Machu Picchu. Find the answers to four of these questions. Share your information with your classmates.

   1. Where is Machu Picchu located?
   2. When was it built?
   3. When was it rediscovered?
   4. Who rediscovered it?
   5. What does "Machu Picchu" mean?
   6. Who lived in Machu Picchu?
   7. What was Machu Picchu used for?
   8. What remains there today?

2. Use the Internet to learn about of these ancient sites. Find out where each site is located and when it was built. Give a short description of each site. Share your information with your classmates.

The Parthenon, Great Zimbabwe Ruins, Borobudur, Petra, Easter Island, Valley of the Kings, Lascaux, Chichén Itza

UNIT 3

1. Work in a small group. Use the Internet to find out about New Year celebrations around the world. Select one of these cultures. Answer the questions below. Share your information with your classmates.

Australian, Brazilian, Buddhist, Cambodian, Chinese, Greek, Pakistani, South Pacific, Swaziland, Thai, Armenian

1. When is the holiday is celebrated?
2. What foods are prepared?
3. What is a traditional way in which the New Year is celebrated?

2. For Hindus, the lotus flower is the symbol of Lakshmi. Flowers and plants have a great symbolic value to cultures around the world. Use the Internet to research the symbolic meaning of one the following flowers and plants. Share your information with your classmates.

carnation, chrysanthemum, daisy, honeysuckle, iris, jasmine, lily, rose, sunflower, violet.

UNIT 4

1. Work in a small group. Use the Internet to find out about Grimm's Fairy Tales. Choose one of the tales and tell the story to tell your classmates.

2. The earliest known form of Arabic literature is the *qasidah* (ode). Use the Internet to look up *qasidah*. Find the answers to these questions. Share your information with your classmates.

1. How many lines are in a *qasidah*?
2. What does this poem usually describe?
3. Into how many parts is the poem divided?
4. What is each part about?

 **UNIT 5**

1. Use the Internet to learn about one of these UNESCO World Heritage Sites. Answer the questions below. Share your information with your classmates.

    Butrint, M'zab Valley, Iguazu National Park, Great Barrier Reef, Royal Palaces of Abomey, Mogao Caves, Mystras, Fatehpur Sikri, Tongariro National Park, Ha Long Bay

    1. Where is the site located?
    2. What is the site like?
    3. Why is it important to the world?

2. Use the Internet to find out about one of these explorers. Then answer the questions below. Share your story with your classmates.

    Harriet Chalmers Adams, Richard Byrd, James Cook, William Dampier, Samuel Meriwether Lewis, David Livingstone

    1. When did the explorer live?
    2. What famous exploration did the person do?
    3. When and where did this happen?
    4. What hardships did the explorer experience?

 **UNIT 6**

1. Work in a small group. Use the Internet to learn about hairstyles in one decade of the 20th Century. Give the name of the hairstyle and describe it. Find pictures if you can. Share your information with your classmates.

2. Use the Internet to find traditional clothing and hairstyles in one of these countries. Answer the following questions. Share your information with your classmates.

    Japan, Ethiopia, India, Jamaica, Peru, Samoa, Holland, Iceland

    1. What is traditional clothing like in the country?
    2. What are traditional hairstyles like?
    3. What do these traditions tell us about the people?

UNIT 7

1. Work in a small group. Use the Internet to find out which came first: the knife, the fork, or the spoon. What was this utensil first made of? When was it first used? Share your information with your classmates.

(continued)

2. Use the Internet to find a recipe for your favorite meal. Write down the ingredients you need, how to cook them, and how to serve your meal. Share your recipe with your classmates.

UNIT 8

1. Work in a small group. Use the Internet to find a traditional wedding custom in one of these countries. Describe what the custom is and what it means. Share your information with your classmates.

   Brazil, China, Egypt, Fiji, Hungary, India, Italy, Morocco, Norway, Russia

2. Imagine you are planning a wedding for yourself or someone else. Use the Internet to find tips on planning the perfect wedding. Make a list of 10 things to do when planning a wedding. Share your information with your classmates.

UNIT 9

1. Work in a small group. Use the Internet to join an archeological dig. Decide what dig you want to participate in and answer these questions. Share the information with your classmates.

   1. What country are you going to?
   2. What site are you going to be working at?
   3. How long will you be away?
   4. What kind of clothes will you wear?
   5. What kind of tools will you use?
   6. What kinds of jobs might you do?
   7. What will you look for?

2. Use the Internet to learn about ancient Egyptian culture. Answer one of these questions. Share the information with your classmates.

   1. Where did the ancient Egyptians build their homes and what did they use to build them?
   2. What rights did Egyptian women have?
   3. What trades did boys learn?
   4. What foods did Egyptians eat and how were they cooked?
   5. What clothing, cosmetics, and hair styles did they wear?
   6. How did they entertain themselves?
   7. What did they believe about their pharaohs?

 **UNIT 10**

1. Work in a small group. Use the Internet to find out about one of these destinations. Find out where the place is located and what there is to see and do. Share your information with your classmates.

   Grand Canyon, Lake Wakatipu, Victoria Falls, Taj Mahal, Nijo Castle, Iguazu Falls, Kruger National Park, Stonehenge

2. Use the Internet to research one of these famous climbers. Find out when and where the person was born and what he or she achieved. Share your information with your classmates.

   Cathy O'Dowd, Ang Rita Sherpa, Achille Compangnoni, Reinhold Messner, Armando Aste, Una Cameron, John Ewbank

 **UNIT 11**

1. Work in a small group. Use the Internet to learn about one of these great people of the Renaissance. Find out where and when each person was born and what he or she accomplished. Share your information with your classmates.

   Sophonisba Anguissola, William Byrd, Vittoria Colonna, Albrecht Durer, William Harvey, Margaret of Austria, Christopher Marlowe, Pierre de Ronsard, Catarina van Hemessen, Andreas Vesalius

2. Use the Internet to learn about one of these explorers. Answer the questions below. Share your stories with your classmates.

   Christopher Columbus, Bartolomeu Dias, Sir Francis Drake, Vasco da Gama, Ferdinand Magellan, AmerigoVespucci

   1. What region did the person explore?
   2. When did this happen?
   3. Who went with the explorer?
   4. What difficulties were encountered?
   5. Did the explorer achieve a historical "first"?

 **UNIT 12**

1. Work in a small group. Use the Internet to find out how, where, and when one of the following sports got started. Share your information with your classmates.

   baseball, basketball, luge, skateboarding, snowboarding, tennis, windsurfing

(continued)

2. Use the Internet to learn about one of these sports figures. Find out where and when each person was born, what sport he or she played (or plays), and what made (or makes) this person famous. Share your information with your classmates.

Yao Ming, Nadia Comaneci, Johan Cruyff, Eddie "The Eagle" Edwards, Billie Jean King, Chen Lu, Catherine Ndereba, Michael Phelps, Hideki Matsui, Shaun White

UNIT 13

1. Work in a small group. Use the Internet to learn more about Australia. Find the answers to two of these questions. Share the information with your classmates.

   1. Why is Australia called "The Land Down Under"?
   2. What is the "Outback"?
   3. What is the size and population of Australia?
   4. What is the climate in its various geographic areas?
   5. Who were the first people to inhabit Australia and what happened to them?
   6. When did Australia become independent from Britain?
   7. What are some interesting plant and animal species found there?

2. Use the Internet to research the lives of the first settlers to Australia OR America. Answer these questions. Share your information with your classmates.

   1. What sort of housing did the settlers have?
   2. What was the weather like?
   3. What did the settlers eat?
   4. How did they get food?
   5. Did the settlers have trouble with native people?

UNIT 14

1. Work in a small group. Use the Internet to learn about the Chinese Tea Ceremony. Find the answers to one these questions. Share your information with your classmates.

   1. What is the spirit and purpose of the tea ceremony?
   2. Where should the ceremony be performed?
   3. How should the pots and cups be prepared?
   4. How should the tea be prepared, served and drunk?

2. Use the Internet to research coffee. Find the answer to one of these questions. Share your information with your classmates.

   1. Where and when was coffee discovered?
   2. What is the legend about how coffee was discovered?
   3. Where does the word "coffee" come from?

4. Where were coffee beans first roasted and brewed as they are today?
5. When did coffee spread to Europe?
6. What is typical Viennese coffee?
7. What country was the biggest producer of coffee in the 19th and 20th centuries?
8. In what climate and conditions do coffee beans grow best?

UNIT 15

1. Work in a small group. Use the Internet to research a remote area. Choose one of the places from the list. Find the answers to the questions below. Share your information with your classmates.

   Amazon Rainforest, Northern Siberia, Sahara Desert, San Blas Islands

   1. What is the climate in this area?
   2. How many people live there?
   3. What group or groups of people live there?
   4. What are their traditional foods, clothes, and houses?

2. Use the Internet to research one of these travelers and explorers. Find the answers to the questions below. Share your information with your classmates.

   James Cook, Jacques Cousteau, Mary Kingsley. Thomas Edward Lawrence, David Livingston, Beryl Smeeton

   1. When and where did the person live?
   2. Where did he or she travel?
   3. Why is he or she famous?

UNIT 16

1. Work in a small group. Use the Internet to find out about one of these famous names in computer technology. Find out where and when the person lived and why he is famous. Share your information with your classmates.

   Paul Allen, John Backus, Sergey Brin, Larry Ellison, Bill Gates, Steve Jobs, Jack Kilby, Pierre Omidyar, Konrad Zuse, Jerry Yang

2. Use the Internet to find definitions for two of the following computer terms. Answer the questions below. Share your information with your classmates.

   boot, browser, bug, chat, cursor, database, drive, file, function keys, hardware, hypertext, language, memory, mouse, network, processor, program, software, user

   1. Do the terms have other meanings that are not related to computer technology?
   2. Are there other ways the words can be used? If so, how?

MAP OF THE WORLD

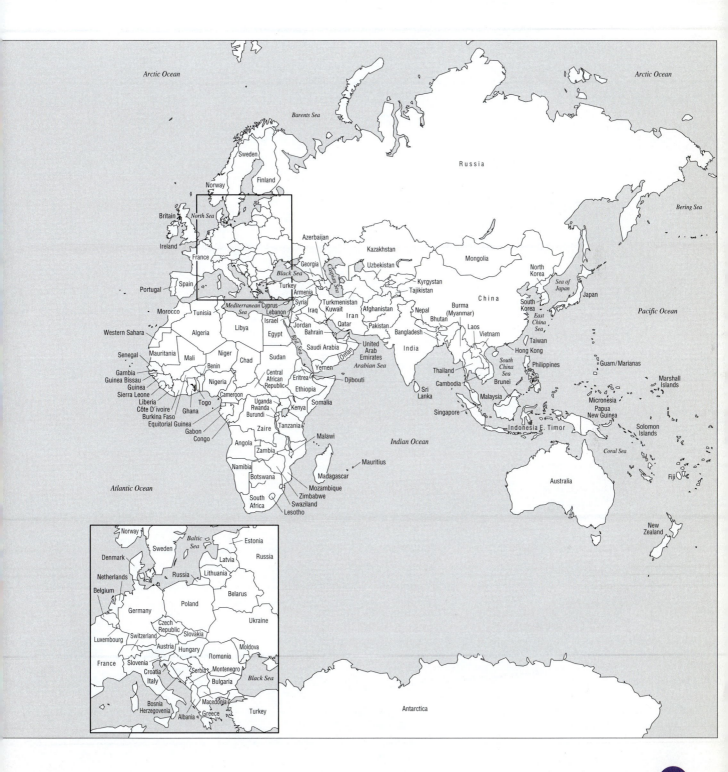